PUB WA

IN

South Cumbria
Westmorland and Furness

Alan Shepley

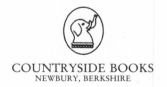

COUNTRYSIDE BOOKS
NEWBURY, BERKSHIRE

First Published 1995
© Alan Shepley 1995

COUNTRYSIDE BOOKS
3 Catherine Road
Newbury, Berkshire

ISBN 1 85306 330 4

Designed by Mon Mohan
Cover illustration by Colin Doggett
Photographs and maps by the author

Produced through MRM Associates Ltd., Reading
Typeset by The Midlands Book Typesetting Company, Loughborough
Printed by Woolnough Bookbinding Ltd., Irthlingborough

Contents

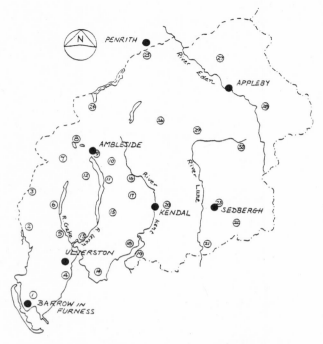

Area map showing locations of the walks.

KEY TO SKETCH MAPS

.... Walk route and suggested direction

Road — River Bridge — Unfenced Road — Canal

■ Building

✝ Church or Chapel

Broadleaved Woodland ♀♀♀♀♀♀♀ Coniferous Woodland

Mixed Woodland

Lake or Reservoir

Dam or Embankment

Quarry or Cliff edge

┼┼┼┼┼ Railway
— + — + — Old Railway
— · — · — County Boundary
— × — × — Fence
▬▬▬ Wall

FB Footbridge
P   Car Park
▲   Summit

Publisher's Note

We hope that you obtain considerable enjoyment from this book; great care has been taken in its preparation. However, changes of landlord and actual closures are sadly not uncommon. Likewise, although at the time of publication all routes followed public rights of way or well-established permitted paths, diversion orders can be made and permissions withdrawn.

We cannot be held responsible for such diversion orders and any inaccuracies in the text which result from these or any other changes to the routes nor any damage which might result from walkers trespassing on private property. We are anxious that all details covering the walks and the pubs are kept up to date and would therefore welcome information from readers which would be relevant to future editions.

Introduction

The present county of Cumbria divides conveniently along a line running south-west to north-east from the mouth of the river Duddon and past Penrith. This book covers the area south and east of that line (a companion volume covering the north and west of the county is in preparation) and includes part of the Lake District National Park, the Shap and Howgill Fells, the upper Eden Valley and that part of the Yorkshire Dales National Park which lies within Cumbria, as well as the country round the head of Morecambe Bay; essentially the existing districts of Barrow and South Lakeland and part of Eden district. More simply, it covers the former counties of Westmorland and Lancashire beyond the Sands – Furness, High and Low – with the Sedbergh area of Yorkshire.

The mountainous nature of much of the area confines the villages and hamlets, and the roads which link them, and results in considerable gaps between pubs. The whole of the Duddon valley, for instance, only has one hostelry, and both the Kentmere and Longsleddale valleys have none at all. The distribution elsewhere has been affected by historical accident – the countryside immediately east of Kendal, for instance, has been a stronghold of Quakerism and so has many hamlets which have no pub. I have endeavoured, therefore, to choose those included on the basis of the attraction of their offerings and the linked walks, as well as geographical distribution. This still leaves a great many which will deserve the attention of your own explorations.

All of Cumbria's landscapes are here, from the coast to the highest fells. Some of them are unique nationally, and even internationally, and the very large proportion of the area which is specially designated in some way only emphasises that fact.

Each of the walks has been re-walked during the preparation of this book to ensure that the route details given are as accurate as possible. You should keep in mind, however, that the countryside is a workplace as well as a leisure resource and the consequent changes, legal and illegal, are surprisingly frequent. It is wise to carry the Ordnance Survey 1:50 000 map sheet for the area as a means of checking the route where you find it unclear on the ground; the appropriate sheet number is indicated for each walk. Talking to local people who live along the way not only helps to keep you on the right track but also often provides additional snippets of information which enhance a pleasurable outing.

The length of time it takes to complete a walk will, clearly, depend on how used you are to walking, the weather, whom you are walking with and the diversions you choose to make. The distance given will be no more than a rough guide to time. Most routes have been chosen with half a day's walking in mind, but there is plenty of scope for adding to them yourself or for linking two of them to make a full day out, and for museum and site visits.

The weather of Cumbria is notoriously unpredictable and, especially amongst the higher fells, proves to be lethal from time to time. Effective rainproof clothing and footwear designed for walking in the countryside (lightweight shoes and trainers are most unwise) are essential at all seasons.

Just as variable as the countryside are the licensees and landlords of the pubs and each will have their attitude to your own food, children, dogs and leaving your car in their car park while you go for a walk. Their views have been indicated wherever practicable but where there is no comment, you will need to ask on the day. Change of landlord and tenant occurs from time to time and it may well be that the person I spoke to has now left so polite enquiry is always worthwhile in any case.

All of the pubs serve food as well as drink and I have indicated the sort of menu which is currently on offer. Once again, variation is quite wide and it should be possible for you to choose one to suit your taste as well as your inclination for a walk. Policies on change of menu often differ from pub to pub; some change frequently, others have built a reputation on a consistent offering. Flexibility of opening hours these days makes planning a day out much easier than it used to be. To enable you to check on up-to-date detail the telephone number of each pub has been included in the description.

I have walked these ways with great pleasure for most of my lifetime and have found the change of the seasons, the variety of wildlife, and the links with our ancestors to be met along the way re-creative in a very real sense. Passing our countryside on to future generations in a better state than we ourselves found it seems to me the least care we can exercise. Please, always, remember the Country Code and encourage others to do likewise.

The ability to express thanks adequately is for ever lacking. Family and friends (four, as well as, two-footed) have shared the joys of walking these paths through the years and have brought so much more pleasure to me through their own response to this superb countryside. Landlords and licensees of the pubs have willingly given me information about their pub, and much else besides. All of them deserve my grateful thanks as do those many briefly-met folk who shared a 'crack' with me along the way. May you, too, find you have "an eye to perceive and a heart to enjoy"!

Alan Shepley
Spring 1995

Barrow in Furness
The Abbey Tavern

1

The present Abbey Tavern is the substantial remains of a massive hotel, built on the site of a former 17th century manor house in 1847 by the Furness Railway Company which had, in turn, been created from the gatehouse of the Abbey itself. The hotel closed in 1938 and became the gun-control centre for the air defences of the Barrow shipyards during the Second World War. This was damaged by an air raid and demolished in the 1950s. An archway still spans the northern approach by the gatehouse Lady chapel and the monumental Abbey buildings form a backdrop.

The spacious and high-ceilinged interior of the Tavern is on two levels and has an atmosphere which chimes well with the mediaeval surroundings outside without, in any way, trying to imitate them. Food is available between 12 noon and 2.30 pm and from 7 pm to 9 pm seven days a week. As well as a selection of sandwiches, the snack menu lists the now widely-popular jacket potatoes with a variety of fillings and a burger choice for the children. The main bar-meal menu offers a substantial choice of starters and main courses, including vegetarian meals, and is supplemented each day with a 'specials' board and, on Sundays, traditional roasts. This gives the chef an opportunity to be more venturesome and I have found a tasty lamb khorma made an excellent change from the more frequent Madras curries. Alternatively, you might go for the hot potted shrimps followed by strips of chicken cooked with thin slivers of peppers in a soy sauce with fresh cream.

As a Whitbread house, the bar is well stocked and is open all day, from 11 am to 11 pm during the week and from 11 am to 3 pm and 7 pm to 10.30 pm on Sundays. Whitbread Trophy beer is joined by Boddingtons, with Heineken and Stella Artois lagers, both Guinness and Murphy's stout, and Bulmer's Original cider. The upper part of the interior is regarded as a non-smoking area whilst families are welcome throughout. The beer garden adjoins the chapel ruins and provides an opportunity to eat your own food with your drinks, should you so wish.
Telephone: 01229 825359.

How to get there: Follow the English Heritage signs from the Dalton in Furness by-pass on the A590 and opposite the hospital on Abbey Road.

Parking: A large car park behind the pub serves both the Abbey Tavern and visitors to Furness Abbey itself.

Length of the walk: 5 miles; reduced to 4½ miles if the alternative route over Bow Bridge is used. Map: OS Landranger 96 Barrow in Furness and South Lakeland (inn GR 218719)

The ruins of Furness Abbey lie in the dramatic setting of the sinuous Vale of Nightshade and are the very substantial remnants of one of England's greatest Cistercian houses. Beyond them, the walk continues down the valley and then climbs up onto the limestone plateau of Low Furness and heads north to the former capital of the area, Dalton. The old town centre is extremely attractive and much quieter since the building of the bypass. The return route, down the valley, follows the meadows and woods which once supplied the local needs of the Abbey.

The Walk

Leave the Tavern and cross the car park to the Abbey ruins. There is now a small museum at the entrance operated by English Heritage. Much of the lay-out can be seen from the footway along the lane as you walk by the fence towards the local car park and toilets at the south of the Abbey ruins. Cistercian monks arrived here in 1127, via Tulketh near Preston, and stayed for 410 years. The Abbey grew rich on extensive lands in Furness, Borrowdale, and farther afield, as they ranched sheep and mined and smelted for iron in the surrounding limestone. As late as 1500 they were still adding to the buildings and the massive square tower represents the final addition.

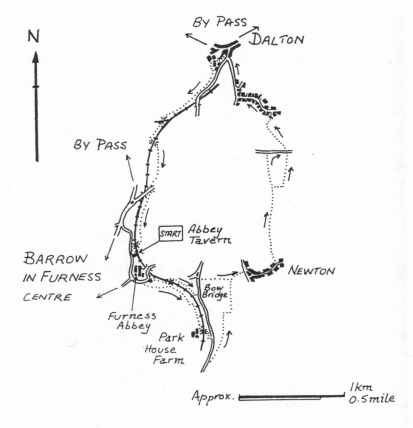

Beyond the Abbey there is a choice of routes. The suggested route leaves the small car park through an iron gate beside the toilet block and crosses the field to the left to parallel the railway and climb up the bank where the path crosses the stone wall of the former Abbey park. The edge of the housing of Barrow is visible up to the right. Continue forward to the stile to the left and follow the signs to drop back down to the valley bottom at Park House Farm. Enter the yard and turn to the left under the railway through a tunnel before the farm access track and join this on the far side; turn left to the lane and then walk to the right for about 300 yards to a sign to 'Newton' on the left which indicates a clear grassy path angling up the bank and up the valley once more. At the edge of the trees, half-left, the stream is spanned by the 15th century Bow Bridge. At the concrete loading platform of the old quarries above, turn up the bank on a track and curve up left to a stile. Cross to the iron gate on the right just beyond the telephone line.

As a shorter alternative, it is possible to continue beyond the car park along the lane to the sandstone building, on the right beside the railway. A path leaves the road (there is no sign) between the building and the embankment and goes under the railway to continue on the far side to Bow Bridge. Cross the bridge and walk up to the lane and turn left to the triangle at the junction. A path on the right goes straight, and steeply, up the bank to rejoin the main route at the gate at the top of the field. From this point the main fells around Coniston come into view.

Walk down the field to the lane opposite the Village Inn, in Newton. Pass the front of the pub and bear to the left and continue along the street of limestone houses past the memorial and Village Hall to the Post Office; which is, unusually, in the Farmer's Arms pub. At the far end of the car park take the path to the left on Long Lane between high hedges. To left and right are ponds which now occupy the sites of the shallow early mines from which iron ore was extracted. Follow the track to a right-angle bend. It is possible here to either continue ahead over the stile and turn right along the road or, as the locals do, to keep with the track and right angle for a second time to reach the busy road.

Cross directly over and follow a footpath beneath a tunnel of hedges. Keep with the right-hand boundary to descend along the edge of the estate until you reach a children's play area. Turn left and left again in 20 yards and cross over to use the footway through the estate past Dalton Primary School to emerge onto the road opposite the cemetery. Drop down Cemetery Hill to the right. Go directly across the main road at the bottom and use an asphalted path which zigzags up the hill to enter the old town square beneath an archway. The Victorian fountain and the baskets of flowers set off well the surrounding cottages and the 14th century pele tower (usually referred to as 'Dalton Castle'), which served as a prison. The church itself is a Victorian replacement for an earlier one and uses the red sandstone and white limestone to good decorative effect.

Back on Church Street, turn to the left past some attractive Georgian façades and drop steeply down the bank to a path on the right by the river, beyond the Brown Cow Inn. Follow the sign 'Millwood' and use the kissing-gate to the left in 50 yards across the Poaka Beck. The path follows beside, and below, the road and railway and then turns below the latter. Towards the main road some of the fields are used for pony grazing.

At the road, go straight across, on the path marked 'Furness Abbey'. The path drops down a little and runs along with the railway now on the right until it passes below it by a small tunnel. In about 50 yards you emerge onto the lane by the Abbey gate and the pub.

2 Broughton in Furness
The High Cross Inn

Whichever your approach route to the High Cross Inn, because it stands almost alone on the neb of a low ridge between Broughton in Furness and the Duddon valley, it is unmissable. An old carters' inn, rather than a coaching inn, it served refreshment after the struggle up from the Duddon crossing. The older part of the building dates from 1660. The comparatively modern addition contains the restaurant which commands the stunning views down the estuary to Walney Island and inland to Coniston Old Man and the surrounding fells.

Inside, the High Cross is airy and spacious and the joins between old and new seem almost seamless. Their speciality is genuine home cooking and the menu is, consequently, a genuine moveable feast! Situated, as they are, within sight of the sea, seafood – lobster, prawns, halibut, sole, salmon – is a staple, and they make a much better offering to the vegetarian than most. This said, the menu for the meat-eating majority remains extensive and the steak pie is justly sought after. Precede this with, perhaps, mushrooms in garlic mayonnaise and follow with a sweet from the trolley and you will be well satisfied. Food is served between 12 noon and 2 pm each day, between 6.30 pm and 9 pm Mondays to Thursdays (9.30 pm on Friday and Saturday), and between 7 pm and

8.30 pm on Sundays.

The bar is open daily from 11 am to 11 pm (10.30 on Sundays) and, as a freehouse, a wide range of drink is available. Webster's Yorkshire bitter and Ruddles County, are complemented by Courage Chestnut mild. Guinness is on draught together with Foster's and Miller's lager; cider drinkers are catered for by Strongbow and Woodpecker. If you want something stiffer for a cold day the selection of malt whiskies is extensive.

The beer garden has more extended views than the restaurant and is adjacent to a play area for the children; consumption of your own food, with the purchase of drinks, is possible in this outside area. Families are welcome, as are well-behaved dogs. The restaurant is maintained as a non-smoking area. En-suite accommodation is available.

Telephone: 01229 716272

How to get there: Follow the A595 north from Barrow in Furness or join this road from the A5092, which links to Greenodd on the A590 from the east. The pub stands on top of the hill on the corner of the road into Broughton in Furness from the west.

Parking: There is a large car park at the pub; please inform staff before leaving cars unattended.

Length of the walk: 2³/₄ miles. Map: OS Landranger 96 Barrow in Furness and South Lakeland (inn GR 207876).

This is an easy and short circuit through farmland and the park of Broughton Tower, followed by an opportunity to look closely at the fascinating small market town of Broughton in Furness.

The Walk

Begin the walk by carefully crossing over the A595 by using the traffic island and drop down the hill on the far verge in the direction of Millom. A footpath is signed to the right in about 250 yards. After a short stretch of field it passes between overgrown hedges and can be a little difficult for a short way if it has not been recently cleared. When you reach the corner of a wood the grassy lane is frequently used by the farmer and is easy going past a young spruce plantation on the left as far as a field gate. The view ahead is of the fells around Coniston Old Man and down to the left are the drained fields of the former moss lands of the river Lickle. Move ahead along the right-hand boundary and alongside a third wood and go right through the steel gate at the far end. Aim diagonally to the left of the farm buildings up the slope to steps and a gate in a small shelterbelt. Turn right on the farm track and pass the buildings

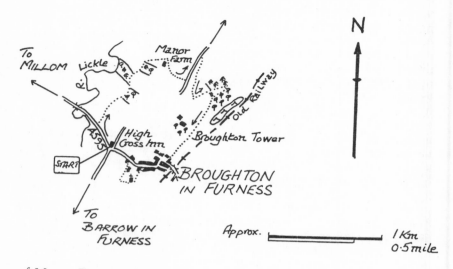

of Manor Farm to the access track and walk up this to the road. Turn to the left and follow the road up around the bend with some care for oncoming traffic. At first you are beside the wall of Broughton Tower estate, with its limestone capping, and then below a high-grown hedge and larger trees to a stile on the right.

Turn hard back on yourself at about 60°, jump the drainage ditch, and contour round the bottom of the slope below the wood through the parkland grazing. At the old access drive, with its locked gates with their tall posts to your right, go left to the iron fence and gate. Just over the fence is an elaborately covered drinking well for the cattle marked 'JS' and dated 1871. 'JS' was J. Sawray who then owned Broughton Tower. You can get a first glimpse of the tower by leaning over the gate. Turn to the left along the iron fence and walk up a shallow valley beside the mixed plantation of spruce and pine on the left. Pass through the gap in the wall and continue towards a wall gap in the corner of the field. Walk to your right along the wire fence before reaching the corner and rise back up the field above broadleaved woodlands covering a steep bank which drops down to a lake in the bottom on the left. Cross a stile and follow the old, grassy wall line on the left and bear gently down the slope leftwards.

Across the lake you can make out the line of the former Foxfield to Coniston branch railway line which opened in 1859. It closed for passenger traffic in 1958 and finally closed completely in 1962. On the right is a much better view now of Broughton Tower. The Broughton family forfeited their lordship in 1487 having taken the losing side in the rising of Lambert Simnel against King Henry VII. Much of what you see is mid-18th century construction by the Sawrays around a 14th century pele tower. The buildings are presently in use as a special school and this is the nearest you can get on a public right of way. Continue down to the edge of the ditch around the wood beside a small games field and walk along it to pass below a high wall to an old iron turnstile gate. Pass between the children's playground and the sports field and bear right along a lane to reach the Market Place past the toilets.

It is well worth taking a complete tour round the square. Begin by going up to your right. In the centre is an obelisk which commemorates the jubilee of George III, in 1810, and close beside it are the town stocks and the fish slabs shaded by tall horse chestnuts. Many of the buildings round the square are Georgian, and often of three storeys. The pattern of the whole was laid down in the style of a London square by Gilpin Sawray in 1760, after a visit to the capital. Dr Oliver, who invented the famous dry biscuits, moved to Bath from here, and Branwell Brontë, brother of the literary sisters, was a tutor to the sons of the Postlethwaite family. On the south side is the Town, or Market, Hall with seven bays which have been filled in but which formerly housed shops; the Information Centre is now located there. At noon on 1st August each year, the Elizabethan Charter is read aloud to the assembled company from the steps of the obelisk and refreshments are given to the townspeople by the Lord of the Manor (now the County Council).

Return to the south-west corner of the Market Place and walk down Griffin Street, past Cobblers Cottage of 1672, and bear right up Church Street at the bottom. Cross over to walk down the side of the old school building to the church of St Mary Magdalene with its clock face bearing the legend 'Watch, for ye know not the hour'. The manor of Broughton was once part of the estate of Earl Tostig of Northumbria (who fought against King Harold at Stamford Bridge, in Yorkshire, before the long march south to Harold's defeat at Hastings). The first chapel on this site seems to have been built soon after to look down across the border into what was then Scotland, across the river Duddon. Much of the fabric was erected when Broughton became a parish in 1547 but the tower is a surprising re-building of 1900.

Remember (in summertime at least) to 'please close the door to keep the swallows out', and exit from the churchyard by the kissing-gate west of the tower. Cross the narrow field to a second gate and turn right along the far side of the hedge to pass some cottages and reach the road again by Syke House, dated WC 1739. Just below, and across the road is Old Syke House, dated ADE 1655 and 'rebulded' (sic) 1740. Walk up the hill back to High Cross.

3 Seathwaite
The Newfield Inn

For many years the Newfield Inn has been the only pub in the Duddon valley (also known as Dunnerdale). Rather than having the effect of causing the proprietors to rest on their laurels the opposite has been the case and folk will travel many miles – you have to! – for the pleasure of food and drink here. The patterned flagstones of the bar floor came out of the immediate landscape and much of the inside has changed little in four and half centuries of use. Some of the beams are reputedly re-used ships' timbers.

Food is served between 12 noon and 2.15 pm, and between 6 pm (7 pm on Sundays) and 9 pm each day. This isn't the place for fancy menus and presentation but it is well-focused on the needs of the walker for good food at reasonable prices. The evening menu provides a range of starters not available at lunchtime so you have to plan a little if herrings in Madeira sauce or potted shrimps stimulate your taste-buds. The Cumberland sausages (in the plural here) make a good, filling dish for most days of the year in this rather damp spot, and vegetarians will find they have a choice. Half portions are served for the children.

Opening times for drinking are 11 am to 3 pm on weekdays and Sundays, and between 6 pm and 11 pm (7 pm to 10.30 pm on Sundays);

the bar is open all day from 11 am on Saturdays. The full range of Theakston real ales are on draught, together with a couple of 'guest' beers e.g. Marston's Pedigree or Young's of Wandsworth. Both Guinness and Gillespie's stout are available as well as McEwan's and Beck's lagers and Scrumpy Jack cider. The selection of malt whiskies is a good one and an exceptional feature is the choice of Polish vodkas!

Families and their dogs are welcome and there is a beer garden at the rear for those sunny days.

Telephone: 01229 716208.

How to get there: From the south, turn up the valley from the A595 on the eastern side of Duddon Bridge about 1 mile west of Broughton in Furness. The approach from the north and west is much harder, even in a modern car, and requires you to cross the difficult Hardknott Pass, from Eskdale, or the Wrynose Pass, from Little Langdale, respectively. In winter either may be closed by ice or snow.

Parking: There is a limited amount of parking in front of the pub and more behind, with a few further spaces along the lane beyond the church. Making the pub the half-way point of the walk enables you to use parking above Fickle Steps.

Length of the walk: 4 miles. The severe weather alternative adds a further 1½ miles. Map: OS Landranger 96 Barrow in Furness and South Lakeland (inn GR 227960).

WARNING! A severe weather alternative is suggested and should be used, in any case, if you have any doubt about your ability to cope with the river crossing at Fickle Steps. The severe weather alternative is recommended, in all circumstances, for families with young children.

This is a delightful walk with excellent views of Dunnerdale, its woods and plantations, which are particularly attractive in spring and autumn. There is some climbing to do and there is a section which will always be wet underfoot. Part of the walk passes through some of the oldest farmed landscape in Lakeland.

The Walk

Leave the inn by turning up the valley and walk around the corner to the church. This tiny church was rebuilt in 1874 to replace that which Revd Robert Walker ministered from for 66 years before his death in 1802 aged 93. 'Wonderful' Walker was so called for his good nature willingness to help others. The stone beside the porch, now topped by a sundial, is that on which he sat to clip sheep at Gateskell, below Wrynose Pass. His

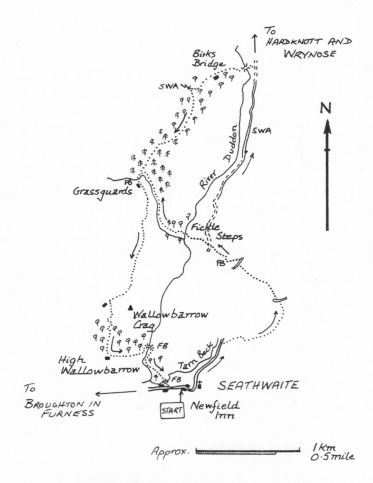

grave is on the right hand of the path from the gate. Continue along the lane and turn first right for Turner Hall. Bear left off the access road on the path signed to High Moss. Swing round below Turner Hall and go left on the obvious track and through the gate beyond and over the field to the isolated house. Walk round to the left of the garden and up the bank to a gate and over the brow to the lane to Long House. Walk left a few paces and go right through the gate to the left of the barn on the corner and follow the right-hand boundary downwards.

Pass through two gates to reach a lane beside the beck on the right. A few steps right brings you to a stile on the left before the bridge. Turn over this and keep the beck on the right to a further stile and a footbridge over the beck. Follow the sign which says 'Alternative drier route' (the straight line is usually a very wet bog) and swing round by the right-hand wall to the bottom of the bank and climb up through further wet patches to an informal car park beside the main valley road. Cross over and drop down a short, steep bank of bracken to Fickle Steps across the river Duddon. If the river is in flood or the steps are icy, or as Wordsworth called it, the river is 'angry Duddon', adopt the following severe weather alternative.

The severe weather alternative (marked SWA on the sketch map) requires you to return to the road and to turn up the valley as far as Birks Bridge with its narrow chasm through which the river roars. Cross the bridge and bear up the bank to the left for the old Birks farmhouse (now an outdoor centre) and continue through on the forestry track to Grassguards where you meet up with the usual route from Fickle Steps (following paragraph).

The stepping stones of Fickle Steps are covered in water when the river is high and the steel hawser stretched across the river is a great confidence booster; the space between some of the steps is a considerable stride. Follow the bridleway to Grassguards up the bank through a rocky wood of beech to a plantation of spruce beside Grassguards Gill. Eventually you reach a heathy area beneath a telephone line with more mature spruces to the right and emerge onto a forestry track. This is where the alternative route rejoins.

Turn left over the ford, or adjacent footbridge, and go through the farmyard of Grassguards. Follow the track south now, between massive walls, and continue past the ruined barns and the 'improved' grazing to the right. Just after the track begins to rise a little and bears to the left slightly, you will find the most massive wall of all on your left. Its height, the thickness, and the size of the blocks all suggest very great age indeed – perhaps over 1,000 years ago. On the skyline of Wallowbarrow Crag ahead are a series of perched blocks.

Turn to the left down the track just before Low Stonythwaite and drop steeply down the stony track below the crag and through the oak wood. Part way down, the track fords a beck and deep red volcanic rocks are exposed on the surface. Continue down through the trees to the farm at High Wallowbarrow in the bottom of the valley. Turn to the left on the National Trust footpath sign immediately you enter the yard and pass the barn to a field. Goats and a friendly Vietnamese pot-bellied pig will often greet you here. Cross the field to a gate into the wood and use either path to reach the river Duddon at the modern, stone-arched footbridge or the stepping stones just below. Bear to the right along the river bank and then keep up a little to the left in about 300 yards to find a second footbridge (over the Tarn beck) and a path which leads through to the road about 100 yards south of the pub.

4 Bardsea
The Bradyll's Arms

Bardsea, as it stands today, is largely a creation of the Bradylls, who re-created Conishead Priory, and the pub is named after the family. It sits, oddly tall, in the angle of what was the main road junction of the village. It appears to have been built as a pub in 1786 by the Gayles, of Bardsea Hall, now demolished, presumably to serve the workers associated with the small port. The bar area still retains its low beams, whilst the restaurant is a modern addition at the rear.

The Bradyll's Arms is well known in the area for its food and a weekend lunchtime may well find it crowded. Service is from 12 noon to 2.30 pm every day, and 6.30 pm to 8.30 pm Mondays to Fridays, 6.30 pm to 9 pm on Saturday and 7 pm to 8.30 pm on Sunday. Starters include Flookborough potted shrimps, from across the bay and, the more unusual, Manx queenies (a small shellfish) with cheese. In addition to the standard offerings of an English pub menu there is the exceptional choice of ten Indian dishes regularly available. A separate vegetarian menu is provided. Salads and a range of sandwiches make up the snack menu for those who prefer not to walk on a full stomach. A special children's menu is constructed around the ubiquitous baked beans and chips.

Opening hours for the bar are 11.30 am to 3 pm and 6.30 pm to 10.45

pm every day (10.30 pm closing time on Sunday). Boddingtons, Timothy Taylors, and Hook Norton provide the standard beers and there will be a guest beer too. The lagers are Stella Artois and Heineken, the stout is Guinness and the cider Strongbow. Draught wines are served and an extremely good selection of whiskies is kept. The restaurant is kept as a non-smoking area. Families are welcome and a children's play area is beside the beer garden. Dogs are welcome in the garden.
Telephone: 01229 869707.

How to get there: Use the coast road, the A5087, from either Barrow in Furness or Ulverston and turn into the village opposite the Country Park; the pub is on the top of the brow on the left.

Parking: A reasonable sized car park is beside the pub. Please check with the landlord before leaving your car there. There is plenty of additional car parking at the Country Park close by.

Length of the walk: 4 miles. Map: OS Landranger 96 Barrow in Furness and South Lakeland (inn GR 300744).

The route climbs out of the village onto Birkrigg Common with its prehistoric stones and fine views in all directions. The circuit is completed through ancient Sea Wood, which runs right down to the shore, and then along the shore itself. The going is easy and dry underfoot.

The Walk
Go left out of the pub door and down the lane past cottages and the modern village hall, in a converted malt kiln, and bear to the right at the bottom to walk through the hamlet of Bardsea Green in its little dry valley; the first outcropping of limestone is here, on the left. Across to the right, on top of the hill, is the so-called 'Mausoleum' – a three-cornered, domed and pinnacled folly built by Col. Bradyll of Conishead. Continue up the bridleway track (there is no sign) between mossy walls and brambles in the hedges and slowly climb up onto Birkrigg Common. At the gate the view is stunning and extends round more than 180°, from north to south. The lighthouse-like structure, on the Hoad above Ulverston, is a memorial to Sir John Barrow, a founder of the Royal Geographical Society; half-right is the folly tower in Conishead Priory park. The Priory itself is now a Buddhist monastery, which can be visited.
   Walk out onto the common with its close-cropped turf, yellow flowered gorse, and swathes of bracken where the soil is deep enough. Continue directly ahead until you reach the unfenced road from Bardsea village. The views around are, perhaps, even better now and the dark

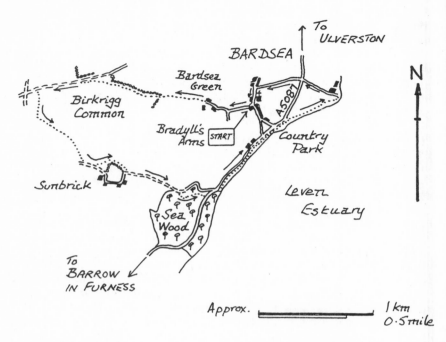

mass of Black Combe towers over the estuary of the Duddon to the west and Coniston Old Man is clear on the northern skyline. Move along the verge for about 50 yards and take an obvious path to the left opposite a right-angle of the wall on the far side of the road. Take a line to the right of a small quarry hole and thread your way amongst the gorse to pass a pair of isolated thorn trees on the crest of the rise. Across to the right you should be able to make out the buildings of High Carley hospital quite clearly and, down below, the crossroads which leads through to Great Urswick.

Eventually you will reach a green track coming up from the corner of the wall by the road from the Urswick side; the view ahead extends down to Walney Island and Barrow in Furness. Turn to the left, up the slope and find the old trig point pillar. A broad, grassy track runs south from here, aiming just left of the large quarry on the far slope of the valley, down to the road. Swing left to parallel the road to drop a little towards the hamlet of Sunbrick. Either go to the left and round the outside of the wall of the field on your own side of the road, or continue down the lane to Sunbrick. Here is the little Quaker burial ground where Margaret (formerly the wife of Judge Fell from nearby Swarthmore Hall), wife of George Fox, was interred. Just beyond Sunbrick, on the left, about 100 yards from the road, is one of several small stone circles on Birkrigg Common; evidence of the interest our ancestors had in this well-drained limestone plateau of Low Furness.

Rejoin the road verge and find a gate into Sea Wood at the top of the hill. The wood now belongs to the Woodland Trust and is full of informal paths on which you may wander at will. The trees are a tangle of oak, beech, birch, ash, elder and hazel and run right down to the sea-shore across the far side of the coastal road. Follow the clear path ahead from the gate and go left at the first crossing of paths to gradually descend through the wood to the road where it bends away from the shore. Take care in crossing and go left along the grass and amongst the bushes on the shore. You are now in Bardsea Country Park, which consists of this strip of shore, almost up to the point. There is an opportunity to go to the right along the shore and look for wading birds, gulls and waterfowl.

About half-way along the Country Park are two buildings on the landward side, one of which was the old mill – now a restaurant. Continue along past the far car park and bear to the right along the top of the shore with its shingle and small patches of salt marsh. Walk along the short sea wall and pass the picnic tables and follow the path over the point of Wadhead. Chapel Island lies just off-shore and the sands of Morecambe Bay stretch out into the distance with the hills behind Lancaster, and even Ingleborough, visible on a clear day on the far side. This part of the shore once formed a small port where the boats were loaded and unloaded at low tide. Drop to the car park by the works and turn to the left up Red Lane – so called from the dust of the iron ore which covered the vegetation as the carts jolted down to the boats.

At the top of the lane cross over the relatively new (1930s) by-pass and climb up the little hill towards the village with the spired church standing out on its knoll up to the left. At the hefty limestone gatepost, on the corner of the village street, go left and walk up to the church. When I last went I met a surveyor carrying out the sad task of assessing the damage which damp has done to this beautifully sited mid-Victorian building. Go left again, on leaving the church, and return to the start.

5 Lowick Bridge
The Red Lion

Lowick Bridge is the most northerly of the Crake valley Lowicks (Lowick Green, and Lowick itself being the others) and little at all shows on the main road. The pub hides just up the lane to the church and looks externally little different from the few surrounding cottages and farmhouses. Its low-beamed interior is surprisingly accommodating and has an air of timeless functionality which is most attractive. Just after the Second World War it was a haunt of Arthur Ransome, author of Swallows and Amazons, and his friends while he was living at Lowick Hall.

Meals at the Red Lion are cooked to order and are worth the consequent slight wait at busy times. Food is served between 12 noon and 2 pm and from 6 pm to 9 pm Monday to Saturday; the later start of 7 pm is made on Sundays. The snack menu is rather more extensive than many, including the substantial 'Lion's bite' double sandwich. Of the main meals the Cumberland game pie (pheasant and venison in brandy and red wine) is something of a local speciality and the specials board carried a toothsome leek and cashew medley when I called in. Children have their own menu as do senior citizens.

A Hartleys (Robinson's) house, the local brew is known as Fellrunners

– though I guess it is more suited to the end of that activity than the start. Guinness and Castlemaine lager are on draught and wine is available. Licensed hours are from 11.30 am to 3 pm and from 6 pm to 11 pm Mondays to Saturdays; on Sundays the bar is open from 12 noon to 3 pm and between 7 pm and 10.30 pm. There is a small beer garden. Your well-behaved dog will be welcome.

Telephone: 01229 885366.

How to get there: From the south, turn on to the A5092 from the A590 at Greenodd and bear right on the A5084 at Lowick Green; the pub is just to the left at the first crossroads. From the north, use the A5084 from the A593 Coniston to Broughton in Furness road and turn right after the sign for Lowick Bridge.

Parking: Parking is limited outside the pub and has to be beside the lane leading to the church.

Length of the walk: 4^1/$_2$ miles. Those who wish to avoid the climb up to the Beacon can shorten the route (S on the sketch map) to 3^1/$_2$ miles. Map: OS Landranger 96 Barrow in Furness and South Lakeland (inn GR 292864).

The fields, woods and fells of the valley of the river Crake are a familiar backdrop for many using the main road to circuit the southern Lakes via Coniston. This walk takes a closer look into this quiet countryside and takes you up onto Lowick Common with its fine views. The walking is quite gentle though it can be a little muddy here and there.

The Walk

Before commencing the route it is worth going left from the pub door and crossing over the main road to lean for a moment or two on the bridge over the river Crake. This is not the usual tumbling Lakeland beck and slides quietly on its way to the sea at Greenodd.

Return to the pub and go up the lane past the houses and turn right on the path signed for Lin Crag and Mill Close. Cross diagonally right to the corner of the wall. On the distant skyline ahead are the slowly turning arms of the generators of Kirkby Moor Wind Farm. Go through the steel gate and cross the beck and aim for the far wall and the stone stile at the right-hand end of it. Walk up the track to Everard Lodge and go right in front of the house and look for the small stile to the left into the wood opposite the corrugated iron sheds. A not too obvious path parallels the edge of the wood through broadleaved trees at first, and then pines and larches, eventually crossing to the right of the boundary

25

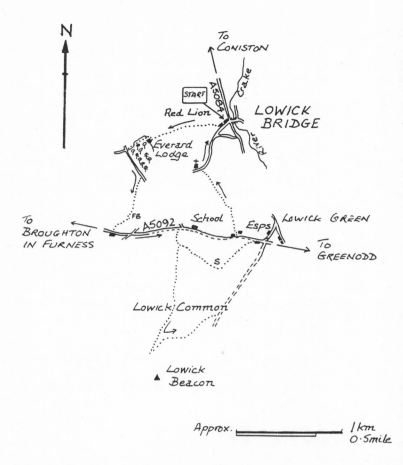

N

To CONISTON

START

Red Lion

LOWICK BRIDGE

Everard Lodge

To BROUGHTON IN FURNESS

FB

A5092

School

Esps

LOWICK GREEN

To GREENODD

S

Lowick Common

Lowick Beacon

Approx. | 1 km | 0.5 mile

wall by a stile. Cross to the corner of the field and exit by the junction of three lanes.

Turn to the left along the lane and the continuation of the wood to pass the entrance track to Everard Lodge and drop a little until you reach a stile to the right over the fence. A few yards further on is the entrance to Lowick Hall, but cross the stile and drop down to ford the beck, lined with mint and globe flower, by the trees on the right. Continue on the same line towards the houses visible in the distance. A scraggy line of alders marks the course of the Langholme beck, beside which grow musk flowers; find the stone footbridge by the wall on the right. Go right through the gate and follow the line of the broken wall on the left to a stile in the wall by the road. Cross over onto the verge by a small footbridge in a bed of nettles opposite Mill Close.

Climb gently up the verge of the main road to the left, past the crossroads, and up to the brow of the hill. For a few yards you must walk on the road and need to take care. Once onto the Common, by the parking bay, you can cross over and walk along the grass verge once again. Continue as far as the 'School' sign on the right and turn right up the path signed to Nettleslack. The track slowly climbs up towards Lowick Beacon and the quarries on Kirkby Moor are clearly visible across the valley to the right. In a groove, rather than a hollow, a path crosses your line. The left-hand, narrower path is the shorter route to Lowick Green (there is no sign) and contours round the side of the hill before crossing a small beck and turning left, more or less parallel to it, and gently dropping to the house by the corner of the Green. If you wish to enjoy the panoramic views from the top, continue ahead to just below the summit. Down to the right is the 100 ft diameter ring cairn of Knapperthaw. The public path angles hard back to the left but there is a permissive path to the very top. Follow the path down, eastwards to reach the unfenced lane just south of Beck Bottom. Geese bred here were once walked to Kendal market with their feet tarred to protect them. Walk along the lane to the Green and rejoin the shorter route. It is worth a gentle amble right round the Green. Until recent times this was an industrial hamlet creating spades, and oak swill baskets, and had two tanneries.

Return to the house at the western corner of the Green and walk along the main road for 100 yards to Esps farm. Turn down through the yard and go left round the silage pit to a gate onto a track. At the three-way footpath sign in the bottom, keep ahead and take the stile by the gate on the left. There is a clear line across the field and up the brow to a stile in the wall and you exit onto the lane at the far side of the next field almost opposite St Luke's church, rebuilt in 1885, with its oddly rusty stones. Sadly, it is usually locked and you may have to go all the way to Penny Bridge for a key. The adjacent field to the west is the site of the local annual agricultural show, which has been held on the first Saturday in September since 1857. Go back past the church and walk along the lane to return to the pub.

6 Torver
The Church House Inn

'The land where the peat was cut' 1,000 years ago has always been a place of more sheep than people and the Church House Inn has been a resort of local and traveller alike for half, or maybe more, of that time. The long, low building shows off the Viking heritage of this part of the world and its beamed interior is no imitation. Though it stands beside the church this latter is only 110 years old and it seems unlikely that the pub's present name is especially ancient, even though the chapel was formerly hard by.

Meals are served in both bars and an à la carte restaurant from 12 noon to 2.30 pm and 6 pm to 9.30pm (9 pm in the winter). There are short, but tasty, separate menus for the vegetarian and for children. Always on the look-out for a local flavour to a meal, I was tempted by the Coniston steak pepperpot with its brandy and peppercorn sauce and a similar approach to making roast chicken a little different was hard to resist. Specials of the day are likely to include both main meals and sweets here.

A Whitbread house, Boddingtons and Castle Eden are the stock ales. Scrumpy Jack cider is on draught as well as Stella Artois and Heineken lagers. Wine is available both on draught and by the bottle. Monday to

Saturday the bars are open all day from 11 am to 11 pm. On Sunday they are closed between 3 pm and 7 pm. The lounge area is especially suitable for families and there is a beer garden at the rear. Open fires are a pleasant feature on cold days. Well-behaved dogs are welcome. Accommodation is available.

Telephone: 015394 41282.

How to get there: The pub will be found in Torver, next to the church beside the A593 Coniston to Broughton in Furness road.

Parking: There is substantial parking at the pub and some additional parking just round the corner in a lay-by beside the A5084.

Length of the walk: 5 miles. Map: OS Landranger 96 Barrow in Furness and South Lakeland (inn GR 284942).

This is quite a gentle stroll around the edge of the two lower Torver Commons and along the shore of quiet Coniston Water (boats are restricted to 10 mph). The shore path is a little rocky here and there but there are no lengthy climbs. Views from the lake shore are especially fine in autumn and bird life is usually abundant on both common and lake.

The Walk

Leave the pub towards the main road junction. This first section of the A593, towards Broughton in Furness, was constructed on the bed of the old railway when it closed, after 99 years, in 1958. The former station is visible to the right as an agricultural dealer's. Cross onto the far verge of the A5084 and walk to the narrow lane to the right on the left of the small campsite, which is signed as a bridleway. Continue along to a junction before Moor Farm and follow the lane between fields, with bird cherry and sloes in the hedges, to a bend with a further bridleway sign to the left for Sunny Bank. An old track passes a lone Scots pine on the left and runs beside the woodland in the ghyll of Torver beck. Over the fence, it is possible to glimpse an old water wheel, and the path drops a little, past Mill House, to Mill Bridge. To the right is Torver Low Common. Turn to the left over the bridge and climb up between hedges to join the A5084.

Go to the right now and pass Emlin Hall, on the other side of the road, and the Land Rover garage. Cross the road to the car parking area and pick up an informal path which parallels the road through the bracken as far as a field fence. For a short distance you must now walk along the road and then turn off on the footpath marked 'Coniston via Lake Shore' by the informal car parking area. The track goes over the brow to a kissing-gate and drops down to the lake shore itself. Through the

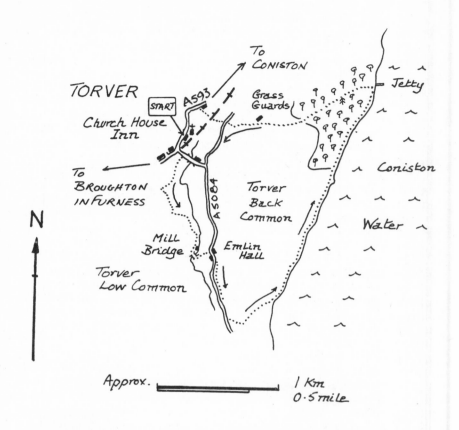

trees to the right you can see Water Park on the far shore. This was the most southerly of the Furness Abbey granges, or sheep ranches, east of Coniston Water in the Middle Ages. The path skirts the edge of Torver Back Common with its scattered trees amongst bracken and gorse.

The whole of this area is National Park Access land and you are free to wander at will – though much of it is a maze of rocky knolls and informal paths. As you reach the shore Dodgson Wood rises up the fell on the far side and the second Abbey grange, High Parkamoor, lies above it. Continue, rising up and down a little over rocky headlands, northwards along the lake shore. Views open up to the north and across the lake to Brantwood (the former home of John Ruskin) and the third Abbey grange, Lawson Park, above it. On a clear day you will see Red Screes, over Kirkstone pass, on the far skyline. Oak, birch, thorn, cherry, rowan, ash and juniper provide cover for a variety of finches, tits and robins. Here and there, bog myrtle - or sweet gale, from which a sort of

30

beer used to be made – scents the air as you cross the little runnels.

At Belman's Hole the view is both up and down the lake and, at the right moment, the stately steam launch Gondola can be seen gliding quietly past with its complement of trippers. For several decades this boat lay rotting on the shore by Water Park but was refurbished by the National Trust and now provides a ferry and trip service on the lake. Eventually you will enter Torver Common Wood through a gate in the fence and find other tree species have now been joined by alders by the shore and the ground is carpeted in mosses. A few tall larches and beeches surround an open grassy area just before a jetty.

At the far end of this forest lawn, turn to the left on the path signed to Torver. Make your way upwards past spruces and through long-abandoned coppices, keeping to the left of the beck. At a gate in the wall is an Access Land sign. Go through the gate and continue along the track. A view up to Dow Crag, the hanging valley of Goats Water, and Bleaberry Haws, on Torver High Common, now opens up. Past the ruin of Grass Guards, you will come to a stile with a dog gate by the farm of Brackenbarrow. Follow the access track to a lane and turn to the left, pass High Stile and, at the T-junction, continue ahead on the footpath across the fields and over the old railway to join the A593 left of the house. As you walk across, Hare Crags dominate the near skyline half-left. On the top is a large ring cairn, one of many prehistoric structures scattered across the Torver commons. Turn to the left along the verge and continue to the church.

The present St Luke's is the successor to a chapel linked to the priory of Conishead, near Ulverston, some time in the late twelfth century. Not until 1538 did it become consecrated ground. In 1861 the Revd Thomas Ellwood, an Icelandic scholar of some repute, became the incumbent. On the way out of the churchyard, and back to the pub next door, notice the walls around the yew trees which have been there since at least 1728.

7 Little Langdale
The Three Shires Inn

The few houses which form the present centre of habitation in Little Langdale surround the Three Shires Inn. The squared faces of the local stone from which the building is made betray its age as little more than 100 years, but it must have had many forerunners, for this is the old route from Ambleside to the coast which served the Romans, then the Vikings, and the pack horses of our more recent ancestors; only since the last War has the road been metalled over the Wrynose and Hardknott passes to the west.

Within recent years the Three Shires has been an all round award winner and it continues to be deservedly popular, especially in the summer months. Food service is between 12 noon and 2 pm and from 6.30 pm to 9 pm in the evening, every day. Summer bar meals are based upon a sensibly restricted menu with sandwiches, ploughman's, and salads to the fore. Hot meals are straightforward and satisfying. A vegetarian dish is always available and there is a children's menu. The specials board indicates the response of the kitchen to current availabilty and seasonal foods. All food is freshly prepared.

As a freehouse, Ruddles County and Webster's Yorkshire ales are always on draught together with a guest beer; Marston's Pedigree, for

example. Foster's and Kronenbourg lagers are kept, as well as Dry Blackthorn cider. The pub is one of those exceptions which keeps a clear non-smoking area inside. The beer garden, beneath its massive spruce tree, has one of the finest views of any. Well-controlled dogs are welcome in the bar but may not be taken into the accommodation and restaurant areas.
Telephone: 015394 37215.

How to get there: Take the A593 towards Coniston from Ambleside and turn right at the sign for Little Langdale beyond the top of the hill from Skelwith Bridge. Alternatively, start the walk from Tilberthwaite which is reached by a lane from the A593, 2 miles north of Coniston, and make the pub the half-way point of the walk.

Parking: There is only a moderate amount of parking at the pub and it is absolutely essential to enquire before leaving your car. The best plan is to use the car parks in Tilberthwaite (GR 307010) or at Hodge Close (GR 316016).

Length of the walk: 5 miles. Map: OS Landranger 90 Penrith, Keswick and Ambleside (inn GR 316033).

WARNING! Families are strongly recommended to walk through the car park area at Hodge Close; there are sheer drops into the quarries by the path on the far side. Care should also be taken in Tilberthwaite Ghyll.

The walk links the 'other' Langdale valley with Tilberthwaite, which does not have a through motor road. The first section is through pleasant National Trust woodlands and this is followed by the exciting narrow chasm of Tilberthwaite Ghyll. The circuit continues through the extensively quarried area around Hodge Close and returns across the fields via the old farm of Stang End.

The Walk
From the pub car park, take the lane 50 paces along to the right marked 'Not recommended for cars', 'Unsuitable for motors' and 'Out of bounds to Army vehicles' – a fairly convincing discouragement to wheeled traffic! This drops down towards the river where there is a raised footway on the right and a footbridge beside the ford. Continue along the track directly ahead and then follow the right-hand fork by the wall to pass the Scandinavian-style hut called Brooklands on your right. At the next fork, bear to the right. The track passes amongst mainly oak woodlands with occasional rushy fields and piles of old quarry waste

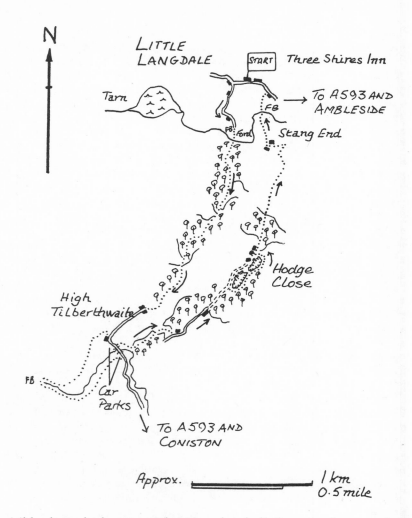

N

LITTLE LANGDALE

START   Three Shires Inn

Tarn

To A593 AND AMBLESIDE

FB

Stang End

FB   ford

Hodge Close

High Tilberthwaite

FB

Car Parks

To A593 AND CONISTON

Approx.   1 km   0.5 mile

visible through the trees. There is a brief climb over a brow and you then drop down through the yard of the farm at High Tilberthwaite.

Continue to the cottages at Low Tilberthwaite and turn up in front of them to pick up the footpath which climbs the lower fellside around the back. Gradually rise and keep to the left-hand path above Tilberthwaite Ghyll on your left. After a while you can cross over the ghyll on a footbridge, and descend, either on a path above it on the far side, or through the profusion of vegetation in the ghyll itself, to reach the car park south of the bridge below Low Tilberthwaite.

Cross the bridge and turn to the right along the river bank (there is no sign) to a kissing-gate into the wood and follow the path through to a track which comes from High Tilberthwaite to the left. Turn right for 20 paces and go left over a stile amongst larches for 50 yards to a field. Walk beside the right-hand boundary and and pass a gate to a telephone pole in the corner by a squeeze stile. Cross diagonally left to a gate which gives access onto a lane by a house. There is a fine view back to the ridges above Tilberthwaite Ghyll. Walk to the left up the lane and through the buildings of Holme Ground with its bank barn. Pass the old quarry cottages on the right and the signed entrance to the quarry on the left and go through the edge of the wood to the track which leads into the car park area beside the old quarries. Families should walk through the car park to rejoin the route at the far end.

Turn to the right by a ruined hut and find a path which bears left again along the edge of the old quarries; part of a complex which once employed over 100 men. The drop is sheer into ice-blue water. This is a popular place for teaching climbing skills and it is a rare occasion to find no one on the rock. Sub-aqua divers also practise in the 100 ft deep pool. The path is edged by heather, bilberry and birch, and gives good views towards the Langdale Pikes and Pavey Ark above Great Langdale. It eventually emerges onto a track after the second large quarry. Go left and turn to the right on the track coming from the car park and pass in front of Wythebank and Wythe How and into woods once more. At the far side the view over nearby Great How is to the Fairfield range.

Go ahead on the footpath (not the track) and bear to the left of the boggy tarn called The Dubs with bell heather and marsh orchids. At the stile bear half-left; there is a glimpse of Little Langdale Tarn to the left. Drop steeply straight down the bank to the access track and turn to the left to the farm at Stang End. On the left, by the barn, are the holes in the wall where the bee skeps (straw hives) used to be kept. The path goes to the right at the gate at the far end of the house and drops down between walls. The view is now open up the valley to Crinkle Crags and Bow Fell. Cross the field to a footbridge over the river Brathay and climb up the field to the left of the house to a gate onto the lane and turn to the left to return to the pub.

8 Grasmere
The Swan

It has been claimed that 14 million visitors come to the Lake District National Park each year. Whether the figure is accurate or not, a very high proportion of them must pass by, and often enter, the door of the Swan, as they have done for over 350 years – both the famous and not-so-famous. Don't be put off by the impact of the rest of humankind. Grasmere has an amazing ability to process them very painlessly indeed and a minor excursion on foot will soon take you away from the crowd.

The Swan serves both bar and restaurant meals between 12.30 pm and 2 pm and from 7 pm to 9 pm in the evening (9.30 pm on Friday and Saturday). The scope is wide and your choice may not be easy to make. What about a salad of marinated meats in a mustard seed dressing, followed by grilled salmon fillet with capers and almonds, and a fine English cheese with an apple to end?

The bars are open from 11 am to 3 pm and from 6 pm to 11 pm Monday to Saturday and from 12 noon to 3 pm and between 7 pm and 11pm on Sunday evening. Beers by John Smith's, Tetley's, Webster's, and Beamish are on draught, with Foster's and Kronenbourg lagers, and Strongbow cider. A wide selection of wines is available. The restaurant is the only non-smoking area. There is a pleasant beer garden. Dogs

are permitted in the comfortable open-fired lounges except during food service times, and also in the public bar.
   Telephone: 015394 35741.

How to get there: The Swan is beside the A591 at the northern end of Grasmere.

Parking: A moderately large car park is situated beside the pub; please check at reception before leaving your car.

Length of the walk: 7 miles. The shorter route (marked S on the sketch map) is 5 miles. The minimum circuit through the village to Dove Cottage and return is 2 miles. Map: OS Landranger 90 Penrith, Keswick and Ambleside (inn GR 339082).

Although the Grasmere and Rydal area justifiably attracts many in its own right as a superb Lakeland landscape it is also the place in which Wordsworth lived, in one property or another, for the last 50 years of his life. The walk takes you to four of these properties – two of which you can visit – and around the shores and along the paths that he knew so well. Making the effort to complete the whole, at least once in a lifetime, is a pilgrimage to the memory of the greatest of the Lake poets.

The Walk
Cross the main road from the hotel and walk along the footway down Swan Lane opposite and cross the bridge over the river Rothay. Turn right on the footpath on the far side of the road opposite the Rothay Garden Hotel into a small woodland belonging to the National Trust. Through the trees the view extends to the pass of Dunmail (where the army of Scotland met its final defeat) with Helvellyn to the right, and to Helm Crag, with its strangely shaped rocks on the crest. At the lane turn left and then go right at the bend beside Glenthorne and take the path signed for 'Score Crag and Easedale'. Follow the path to the left by the large stumps towards the large house on the brow. This is Allan Bank, where Wordsworth lived between 1808 and 1811; it is not open to the public. At the driveway, turn down to the left and walk down to the edge of the village by the telephone boxes.
   For the minimum circuit, go straight ahead and turn into the churchyard by the Grasmere Gingerbread shop. Exit from the far gate to walk along Stock Lane to Dove Cottage at Town End. Return as for the main route.
   For the main route, go right along Langdale Road to the corner opposite the Council car park and garden centre. Turn right again along Red Bank Road and pass the boat hire hut across from the entrance to

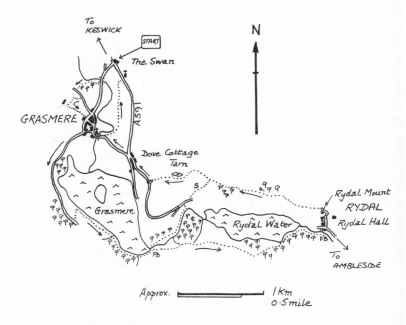

Approx. |————————| 1 Km
0·5 mile

'Kelbarrow'. The road is narrow and care needs to be taken, but you are unlikely to be alone, for this is the only way to reach the lake shore. About 150 yards beyond 'The Lea' a permissive path leads down wooden steps to the left and to the shore of the lake itself. Waterfowl – swans, ducks, and geese – are always about, as are the gulls and the cheerful pied wagtails.Follow the shore path along to woodland edge and to the footbridge by the outflow.

The short route now crosses the footbridge and bears right, through Penny Rock woods, and down river to a gate into a meadow. At the far gate, by the footbridge, turn the other way and walk to the middle of the open grassy picnic area of White Moss Common. Take the path to the left and go up the steps to the main road and cross over with great care. Walk to the right, past the car park in the quarry and turn up to the left on the far side of the beck beside the post box on a pole. The path climbs up fairly steeply to join the main route below the cottages.

To follow the main route bear up to the right to join the bridleway, known as Loughrigg Terrace, and climb a little to a grassy hause outside the wall of the wood. Cross over the top and bear right on a path which contours across the slope of Loughrigg above Rydal Water to pass the top of a second wood. At the head of the lake is a large area of reed bed, now a nature reserve. Gently rise to a rocky brow and pass the slate mines usually referred to as 'Rydal Cave'. Drop down through the larch trees and pass the lower cave and go into the wood and down to fields. Beside the gate there is a fine view up the lake. Bear to the left and zigzag down to a gate into the Rydal Woods above the shore. At the far side of the wood cross a field and take the footbridge left to go up onto the main road opposite the bar of the hotel. Cross the road to the footway and walk round the bend to the corner.

Go steeply up the lane past St Mary's Church on the left. Just beyond, on the right, is the entrance to Rydal Hall, now a Diocesan centre; the gardens are open to visitors. A few yards further, on the left, is Rydal Mount, Wordsworth's home from 1813 to 1850 and open to the public (closed on Tuesdays in winter). A short, steep climb around the bend brings you to a bridleway to the left beyond the car park signed to Grasmere. The route is now, in fact, the old 'corpse road', by which the dead were carried for burial at Grasmere before Rydal had its own church. Walk on to Brockstone cottages above White Moss Common (where the short route rejoins this one).

Continue ahead on the track and, eventually, a metalled lane. On the right is a tiny tarn with a dense growth of mare's tails in summer. Start to drop down the hill; the view ahead is to Easedale, across the valley. Turn to the right opposite the farmhouse at How Top (with the sign in Japanese on its gate). The lane drops down quickly now to the hamlet of Town End where the Wordsworths lived from 1799 to 1808 in Dove Cottage, on the right. This and the adjacent magnificent museum are open to the public.

On leaving Town End, cross over the main road and head for Grasmere village along Stock Lane. Pass the car park and the shops and cafes and cross the bridge to the church of St Oswald. The oldest part of the building is fourteenth century. Inside the beams are open to view and, as Wordsworth put it 'like leafless underboughs in some thick wood'; the outside is plainly rendered. The graves of Wordsworth and other members of the family are on the east side. Leave the churchyard on the north side beside the tiny, Gingerbread Shop – once the schoolhouse. Walk back round the outside of the churchyard; across the road is the Rectory, where the Wordsworths spent unhappy months in 1812–13, and where two of their children died. Recross the bridge and continue to the entrance of the school and take the path through the school yard and pass the Workmen's Reading Room and the edge of the field where the famous Sports are held in August. Go left into the field through the wooden kissing-gate and follow the clear path through the fields to emerge onto A591 opposite the RC church of Our Lady of the Wayside; cross the road and return to the start.

Ambleside
The White Lion

The town of Ambleside has under 3,000 permanent residents but boasts in the region of 14 or 15 pubs. The White Lion is one of the most central and has managed to maintain something of the imposing air of the Georgian coaching-house it once was with its spacious lounge bar and its tall street frontage.

Meals are served from 12 noon to 2.30 pm (noon to 2 pm on Sundays) and between 7 pm and 9 pm. At lunchtimes a range of sandwiches, open sandwiches, toasted sandwiches and ploughman's lunches cater very well for the large passing trade. Sausage, ham, and fish dishes provide for the cold days and there is a choice of vegetarian dishes. The evening menu has an expanded range of starters and hot and cold meals from chicken to steak and from trout to scampi. A pleasant variation is a special afternoon tea menu from 3 pm to 6 pm.

A Bass house, the bars are open from 11 am to 11 pm Monday to Saturday, and from 12 noon to 3 pm and between 7 pm and 10.30 pm on Sundays. Bass bitter and mild are complimented by Worthington best bitter. Lagers are Tennent's, Carling and Pilsner and Guinness is on draught. Ciders are Dry Blackthorn and Taunton Sweet. The dining room is a non-smoking area. Situated, as it is, in the crowded town centre, there is simply no room for any garden but tables on the forecourt provide a pleasant situation to eat, drink and watch the world go by. Accommodation is available. Dogs are welcomed.

Telephone: 015394 33140.

How to get there: Ambleside has a clockwise one-way system, which is notoriously slow at peak holiday times. The pub is across Market Place from the Post Office as you travel south at the point where it is renamed Lake Road (A591).

Parking: A small car park exists behind the pub. It is essential to ask at reception before leaving your car. As alternatives, large pay-and-display car parks are to be found opposite the Charlotte Mason College and at Waterhead.

Length of the walk: 4³/₄ miles. Map: OS Landranger 90 Penrith, Keswick and Ambleside (inn GR 376043).

There are a multitude of delightful walks in the immediate environs of Ambleside. This route provides a circuit around the southern half of the town. There are some pleasant waterfalls in Stock Ghyll, fine views from above Stock Ghyll and from Jenkin Crag, and the walk is completed by visiting some of the historic features of the town.

The Walk

From the front of the White Lion turn hard to the left and walk up Cheapside, in front of the National Westminster Bank, and join Stock Ghyll Lane. Climb slowly up the lane beneath the trees and with Stock beck tumbling noisily down on your left. Take the gate to the left just beyond Stock Ghyll Court and follow the path up as close as possible to the beck. Cross the footbridge and continue up the far bank. There is a right fork, with hand rails beside the path, which leads to a fine view up to the waterfalls; it is a dead end so you must now return to the main path and turn right. Continue and cross the bridge above the falls and go past a picnic table to an iron turnstile which leads back onto the lane.

Go left up the farm access road for about 300 yards and take the steep iron ladder stile up to the right. As you walk up the field the view across the valley is of the steep road up to Kirkstone summit, known as 'The Struggle' because it is, even in a modern car. At the top of the field an up-and-over stile leads onto a walled green lane with some fine ash trees along it. As the lane starts to drop there are some massive old sycamores and larch. At the houses, join Blue Hill Road and go first left on Fisherbeck Lane and then right to a

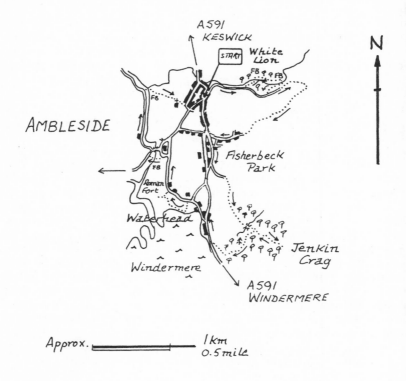

T-junction with Old Lake Road. Walk to the left past Fisherbeck Farm, Lakeland Knitwear, and Hayes Garden Centre, across the car park on the right.

Fifty yards before joining the main road bear up to the left on a metalled lane signed for Jenkin Crag. Climb up between mossy walls and enjoy further views of the Langdales and behind to Dove Crag up Scandale. Join a bridleway by the entrance to 'Strawberry Bank' and contour along the track beyond 'Broad Ings'. The path now enters the National Trust property of Skellghyll Woods. This is a summer haunt of redstarts and pied flycatchers. Look for the sign on the right for Jenkin Crag. An informal path leads out onto a rocky knoll with a stunning view – from Langdale, in the west, to Gummers How, far to the south, down the lake. The whole of the upper lake basin is in view and the central islands, around Bowness, stand out clearly. Return towards the bridge but turn down to the left on the near side of Stencher beck.

The stony path goes steeply down for a short way and then eases off as you come to the gardens at Stagshaw. Cross the car park at the bottom and join the access drive. The gardens are open to the public and are famed for their rhododendrons and azaleas in the spring and early summer. Leave the gardens down the drive and turn right on a footpath opposite the barn on the left. The path leads down to the A591 opposite Waterhead garage. Cross the main road with care and go right along the footway, past the Youth Hostel, and bear down left by the traffic lights, and go down to the steamer pier.

Walk along the small promenade by the boat jetties and the well-fed swans, ducks, and gulls (and, maybe, the occasional rarer waterfowl) and pass the National Park Information Centre and car park. Use the footway round the bend of the road beyond Wateredge Hotel and go left into Borrans Park. A path skirts the shore and gives further views of the lake. Follow this round to a gate in the western wall and cross over the field to the remains of the Roman fort, called Galava, which guarded the road to Ravenglass on the western coast. There have been recent excavations but only outlines of some buildings can be seen in the grass. The reed beds by the head of the lake are a nature reserve. Turn back and go diagonally to the corner, where there is a gate onto the road at the bend. Cross over with care and use the footway to the far corner of the rugby field. Cross back over the road once more and go down the start of the A593 Coniston road, by the hotel. Cross over the river using the new memorial footbridge to the left and turn right to the lane before the roadbridge signed 'Under Loughrigg'. Walk along this, beside the river Rothay with its overhanging trees until you reach the footbridge to the right which gives access to Rothay Park.

Cross the park to the church of St Mary; one of only two in Lakeland with a spire. Built in 1850 there is a mural inside of the rushbearing ceremony, which takes place each year in July (if you miss this one, there is another at Grasmere, in early August). Leave the churchyard at the north-east corner, by the recreation ground, and walk up Compston Road to the town centre. Go left for 50 yards to see the tiny Bridge House (now a National Trust shop), built over the Stock beck. Cross over and look up the beck from the bridge. An old mill still exists on the left – one of five on this beck alone. Continue in front of Central Buildings and pass the market cross on the brow; a market charter was granted in 1650. Over the brow and round the bend, turn to the right under the archway into The Slack and admire some of the older cottages. Take the first left, St Mary's Street, and walk through to Church Street opposite the Wildlife Trust shop. Turn up to the left and cross over to look at the plaque which records where Wordsworth's office was when he was the Stamp Officer for Westmorland on the building just below the bakery; it's now a restaurant. On the opposite corner is the attractive black and white Royal Oak inn. Go past this and return to the start on the far side of Market Place.

10 Troutbeck
The Mortal Man Hotel

The main road from Windermere towards Penrith runs through the valley and yet Troutbeck, within long sight of the teeming crowds of Bowness on Windermere, is still relatively quiet, with its eye focused on earning a living. The building of the Mortal Man has gradually expanded over the years but retains its famous sign by the roadside, originally painted by Julius Caesar Ibbetson some time before 1817.It depicts two local fellsmen with the text:

O mortal man that lives by bread
What is it that makes thy nose so red?
Thou silly fool that looks so pale
'Tis drinking Sally Birkett's ale.

Both restaurant and bar meals are available, the latter between 12 noon and 1.50 pm only, each day. Service in the evening is from 6.30 pm to 9 pm (except for Mondays), and between 7 pm and 9 pm on Sundays. The hotel dining room menu is varied frequently and offers some interesting local fare. A starter of smoked venison and Cumberland ham with herb mayonnaise might be followed by grapefruit sorbet, to clear the palate, ready for pork fillet with Calvados, seasoned with thyme, and finished with cream. Even that rare idea of a savoury final course is available –

how about mushrooms on toast with anchovy butter; a variation well worth indulging yourself with? Children's portions are served.

Beers are Scottish and Newcastle together with the Theakston's range. Guinness stout, Beck's and McEwan's lagers, and Strongbow cider are on draught. A range of house wines is available at the bar and a selection of others in the dining room. Opening hours are from 12 noon to 2.30 pm and from 5.30 pm to 11 pm (7 pm to 10.30 pm on Sundays). The beer garden commands delightful views of the valley. A high standard of accommodation is available. Dogs are welcome on the lead.

Telephone: 015394 33193.

How to get there: Either take the lane signed for Troutbeck and the National Trust property of Town End from the A591 just south of Low Wood, or turn towards Troutbeck from the A592, Kirkstone Pass road.

Parking: There is a large car park available.

Length of the walk: 6³/₄ miles, 1 mile less if Town End is omitted. Map: OS Landranger 96 Penrith, Keswick and Ambleside (inn GR 411034).

Once away from the A592 the valley is quietly rural and most attractive in its detail. The settlement is strung out along the lane half-way up the western slope and there is much evidence to be seen of how a typical Lakeland landscape developed through the centuries. The farm of Troutbeck Park belonged to Beatrix Potter and became the core of the holdings which she bequeathed to the National Trust on her death.

The Walk
Begin your walk along the lane through the village. It is narrow and care should be taken for traffic around the bends. The village is really a collection of smaller hamlets strung out along the lane. The first you come to, beyond Nanny Lane, the track leading up right towards the top of Wansfell, is Longmire Yeat with some fine old barns and chimneys. Beyond Stoneythwaite is the first of three roadside wells – St James', St John's and St Margaret's – built to serve the village before the days of piped water. There is also a fourth, with no name, but dated 1672. Continue past Birkhead, and High Fold, to come to the Institute which has the Post Office in the bottom of it. Just beyond the corner of Green Lane (which leads down to the church) is Thwaite, a recently renovated statesman farmer's house of 17th century vintage.

It is worth walking a further ½ mile along the lane to reach Town End. Here is a superb house, built by the Browne family in 1626 and lived

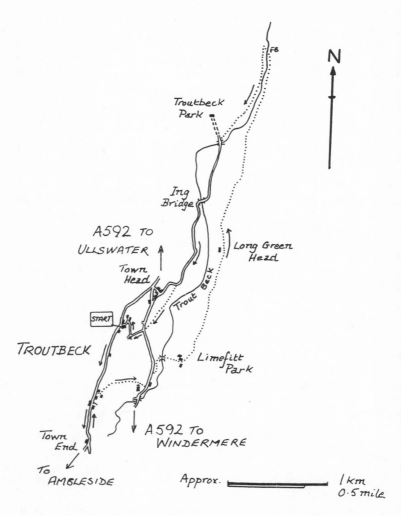

N

Troutbeck
Park ▪

Ing
Bridge

A592 TO
ULLSWATER

Long Green
Head

Town
Head

Trout Beck

START

TROUTBECK

Limefitt
Park

Town
End

A592 TO
WINDERMERE

To
AMBLESIDE

Approx. ▬▬▬▬▬ 1 km
0·5 mile

FB

in by their descendants until 1944. It contains a remarkable collection of
period furniture and household effects: perhaps one of the best places
to begin a close look at the variety of local building styles. It is open
to the public (afternoons only), Tuesday to Friday, Sundays and Bank
Holidays, from April to November. Across the road (and not open to
viewing since it is still in use) is a very fine bank barn with a gallery. If
you have made the diversion to Town End, return now, past the Institute
to High Fold.

Turn through the buildings and take the track down the bank between hedges and some stone-flag fences to a stone footbridge over the Scot beck to a gate into the churchyard. The church is originally 16th century with a tower of 1736 (with a clock of only two faces) and rebuilding in Victorian times as well and is, exceptionally, dedicated to Jesus. Take the opportunity to see the fine east window of 1873 by Burne Jones, William Morris and Maddox Ford. Leave the church by the gate on the A592, cross over the road by the drinking trough, and turn up the hill past the old school of 1637, which is still used as a nursery.

In about 100 yards the entrance to Limefitt Holiday Park has a bridleway sign pointing along the driveway. Go down this and cross the bridge over Troutbeck itself and climb up to the 'Ramblers' bistro and take the path around the back to a green iron gate and go through onto the track. This now contours the eastern side of the valley. As you walk along, the peaks of the ridges will be clearly in view: Wansfell is above the village, Troutbeck Tongue splits the valley into two, and Thornthwaite Crag towers behind at the valley head. Above you are Yoke, Ill Bell and Froswick. There are scattered trees in the bottom of the valley and a substantial wood on Raven Crag across the far side. The pattern of fields is clear, with the oldest, and smaller, intakes around the farms, and the later, larger enclosures (around 1842) up the valley side above. The highest part of the fell is effectively not sub-divided at all. Pass the farm of Long Green Head and continue above the valley bottom fields and cross a small ford below a waterfall in Miles Gill. The path goes by another bank barn on the left and there is a view through the gap up to Red Screes and Woundale on your left. You are now moving into the valley to the right of Troutbeck Tongue, called Hagg Gill, and the route runs below quarries to a footbridge by a barn and a gate in the wall. Cross over and go through the gate and turn immediately hard left to a second gate. This is now a footpath and no longer a bridleway. Follow over the brow and cross the field to the left down the bank past the circular mound of Hall Hill to reach the access to Troutbeck Park Farm at Hagg bridge below the farm itself. This was once the deer park of William de Lancaster.

The lane is surfaced and winds its way along the valley bottom, over Ings bridge. Wild flowers are in abundance on the banks and in the hedges and bird life is ever present by the river and in these sheltered meadows. A badger sett is visible to the keen-eyed at one point. The lane eventually swings up towards Town Head. At the Queen's Head inn here an annual hunt supper keeps up the tradition of more than 200 years. The field beside is where the gallows once stood. Do not climb up into the hamlet but continue ahead on the bridleway under overarching hedges of thorn and rose. At the main road cross over and take the metalled lane ahead and turn first right beside Scot beck. Bear up to the left to return to the start.

11 Windermere
The Grey Walls Hotel

Windermere village is almost entirely a creation of the coming of the railway and many a visitor is still surprised to find that the lake (the 'mere') is not on the immediate doorstep. In the last 140 years or so the tourist has largely taken over the old centre of Bowness on Windermere (which is by the lake) and the local centre has moved uphill to the development around the station. Almost all of the building, until very recently, was in local stone – hence the apt name of the hotel – and new work, even now, is carefully controlled to ensure that it fits in.

The bar of the hotel is, with some wit, named Greys Inn (though its previous existence was as a doctor's surgery, not a legal practice). Food is available from 12 noon to 2.30 pm on weekdays (2 pm on Sundays), and from 5.30 pm (7 pm on Sundays) to 9.30 pm in the evening; service is throughout the day on Saturdays. The menu is an extensive one, with grills particularly popular. Vegetarian, snack, and children's menus are provided.

The range of beers is also quite large with the full Theakston's choice, Thwaites Big Ben, and Youngers Scotch ale. Stout drinkers are catered for with Guinness and Gillespie's and there are no less than four lagers on draught. Draught wines are served and there is a special selection

of the month. Opening hours are from 11 am to 11 pm Monday to Saturday, and from 12 noon to 3 pm and 7 pm to 10.30 pm on Sundays. The TV room serves as a family room and there is a beer garden at the rear. Well-behaved dogs are welcome in the bar. Accommodation is available.
Telephone: 015394 43741.

How to get there: Use the A591 and take the first turn into the village in the Ambleside direction from the station, into Elleray Road; the hotel is on the right.

Parking: There is a medium-sized car park beside the hotel. It is essential to check at reception that you may leave your car. Alternative on-street parking can be found around the edges of the village; the centre is very crowded at holiday times.

Length of the walk: 4 miles. Map: OS Landranger 97 Kendal and Morecambe (inn GR 412986).

There is a quite natural tendency for those who enjoy a quiet walk to separate themselves from the crowds of summer Windermere and Bowness. This is a pity for, as this walk shows, there is much in the immediate surroundings of both beauty and interest. The circuit links both villages and the lake shore, and includes some marvellous views. There is perhaps, in any case, some merit in considering the walk for those mild and sunny off-season days.

The Walk

Make your way from the hotel entrance up Elleray Road to the main A591 and go left, along Ambleside Road and past Phoenix Way and the doctor's surgery (with its ornamented chimneys) to St Mary's church. This was a long time a-building — 1848 to 1882, in various stages. The nave was reroofed in local slate relatively recently after a fire. Sadly, it is another church which is usually kept locked partly, no doubt, because the first lot of roofing slates were stolen the day they were delivered! Cross the entrance of St Mary's Park to a footpath and walk down the walled track between the gardens of large houses. A hydrangea grows up an oak tree beyond Tower House and maidenhair fern clings in the cracks of the walls. On the right, by the cemetery, are some tall Cupressus (Retinosporas) and Western Hemlocks. Go direct ahead to the A592 and cross with care to a National Trust woodland and the footpath signed to Millerground. The tumbling Wynlass beck is bordered by swathes of butterbur.
Across the little bridge you quickly come to the lake shore and the

farmhouse of Low Millerground with its crow-stepped gables. The semi-circular projection on the lake-side houses a spiral staircase and above the barn at the far end a small bell once hung, which was tolled to announce that a ferry was crossing the lake from Belle Grange; a route no longer functional. Precisely how old such houses are is difficult to say; this one could be anything between 1650 and 1750. The view across the lake from the nearby landing stage, by the boat-house, towards the Langdale Pikes is a fine one indeed; especially on a crisp, calm day. Leave the shore now and go through the gate into the field which rises up behind the house and climb steeply to the top. This is Queen Adelaide's Hill and is, today, National Trust property. It was renamed from Rayrigg Bank after Adelaide, Dowager Queen of William IV, visited the spot in 1840 to admire the view. She was already following a long tradition. Thomas West, in the first of the many guide books (1774), wrote 'You will be struck with astonishment at the prospect spread at your feet. . .' – this is no less true today. The additional impact from your previous position at the landing is astonishing: down the lake, to the south, is Gummers How, Claife lies across the water, the Coniston fells, Crinkle Crags and Langdale are beyond, Fairfield stands at the lake head, and the Troutbeck valley runs up to the north-east, down below are the islands of the centre of the lake.

Leave the hilltop in the direction of the lake islands and find a stile in the wall in the left-hand corner and join the path along the wooded shore amongst ash, beech, birch, hazel, holly and rowan with gulls, ducks and swans for company. Find the gate to the left into Rayrigg Meadow and cross over this and to the footway on the far side of the main road and walk to your right. Immediately, you will pass Rayrigg Hall where William Wilberforce, Prime Minister of anti-slavery fame, spent several summers in the 1780s; already he was remarking that the banks of Windermere seemed as public as those of the Thames. Continue along to the bend where Europe's only Steamboat Museum is located. Even if you have no great interest in the technology this is well worth a visit (it is open from Easter to the first week of November). The museum offers trips on the lake in genuine Victorian steamboats, Beatrix Potter's boat, and an example of the old, rowed ferryboats. If you continue on the main road to the far end of the car park by the toilets you will find 'The World of Beatrix Potter' museum, in the Old Laundry, up the steps on the left. Children of all ages will hardly resist the re-created animals from her stories and there is a fine exposition of her life as a Lakeland farmer as well.

Go across the car park to Fallbarrow Road (or walk directly down it if you do not wish to see the Beatrix Potter exhibition) and keep to the right by the entrance of the Royal Windermere Yacht Club and reach the centre of the old village of Bowness on Windermere by the entrance to

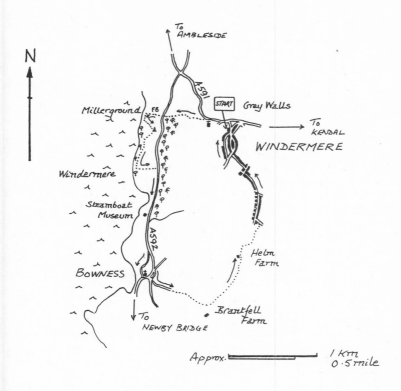

N

To AMBLESIDE

START Gray Walls

A591

Millerground FB

To KENDAL

WINDERMERE

Windermere

Steamboat Museum

A592

Helm Farm

BOWNESS

To NEWBY BRIDGE

Brantfell Farm

Approx. ▭▭▭▭ 1 Km
0·5 mile

St Martin's church. To the left is the New Hall Inn (usually called The hole in't'wall), dating from 1612. The church was founded in the 1200s; much of the present building dates from 1483 and was restored in 1870. The east window may have been moved here from either Furness Abbey or Cartmel Priory and contains the arms of the Washington family. The murals and painted texts are unusual. Beneath the chancel is the grave of 47 members of a wedding party who were drowned when the ferry sank as they returned from Hawkshead, in 1635. If you want a quick glance at the promenade and steamer piers these are just to the right. Otherwise, go out of the churchyard by the lychgate and cross the road to the left and walk round to the bottom of the narrow, pedestrianised Ash Street with several old cottages. Bear to the left at the top of Ash Street into Brantfell Road.

At the bottom, on the left, is the old schoolhouse with its inscription which records that the foundation stone was laid in 1836 by one William Wordsworth. The road climbs quite steeply up (and is here the start – or end – of the long distance Dales Way). On the left is another inscribed stone let into the wall which came from the earlier Applethwaite and Undermillbeck School and is dated 1637. Eventually you enter a field through an iron gate and find a sign which reads 'Ilkley 81 miles'. At the track continue across beside the wood and go more gently up the next field. At the steps, do not go up but bear to the left through the gate. Cross the access to Brantfell Farm, use the kissing-gate and take the left fork of the path.

You are now amongst rocky, wooded, gritstone knolls with much more shortened views. A second kissing-gate takes you through to an area of parkland with tall wellingtonias. Cross the driveway and go to a third kissing-gate. Pass in front of Helm Farm and drop a little to the right through a gate and beside a new plantation of sycamore, oak, ash, and rowan. Take the right-hand path along the wood edge and turn right at the bottom of the field behind the house gardens. Keep on the left-hand of the signed footpaths, which takes you through a rock garden to the top of Lickbarrow Road. Turn to the left, with a final view of the Langdales, and go right to pass the house with the strange pot spheres on its chimneys.

Gently descend past Heathwaite Post Office and Queen's Park – recording Victoria's Jubilee in 1897 – on Park Road and go right at Holly Park House and then left in 50 yards onto Broad Street. The old Council Offices, of 1899, are on the right and the Library and another tall wellingtonia in a small park to the left. At the main road, cross over half-left and walk in front of Jordans 'Corn Merchant, Hay and Straw Dealer' and go right up College Road to the junction with Elleray Road; the pub is a few yards along to the left.

12 Outgate
The Outgate Inn

The countryside which lies between Windermere and Coniston Water is one of infinite variety amongst small rocky hills and extensive woodlands. Its capital, in so far as there is one, is Hawkshead and The Outgate stands beside the main route from there to Ambleside in one of its several outlying hamlets. A beer shop from the late 18th century, it only acquired its spirits licence in the 1950s. For much of the late 1800s barrels were also made here, no doubt from locally grown oak. At the turn of the century they made their own aerated water and later kept stables and sold paraffin.

On the driver's circuit of Windermere, via the ferry or Newby Bridge, the Outgate is an extremely popular pub. Meals are served between 12 noon and 2 pm and from 6.30 pm (7 pm on Sundays) to 9 pm. The grills and salads are especially enjoyed and the snack menu at lunchtime of ploughman's lunches, sandwiches, toasted sandwiches, and filled jacket potatoes is varied. Both vegetarian and children's menus are available. The specials are well worth watching for and I found the steak in beer satisfyingly hard to beat.

This is a Hartleys (Robinson's) house and sells their own good ales, together with Frederic's Premium, Tennent's and Castlemaine lagers,

Strongbow cider, and Guinness. There is no beer garden though there are a few outside tables by the roadside in the summer. The lounge and snug are available for family use. Dogs are welcomed. Accommodation is available.

Telephone: 015394 36413.

How to get there: Take the A593 from Ambleside and turn left onto the B5286 for Hawkshead; alternatively approach from Hawkshead on the B5286.

Parking: A small car park exists behind the pub. Please ask at the bar before leaving your vehicle.

Length of the walk: 3¹/₂ miles. Map: OS Landranger 97 Kendal and Morecambe (inn GR 995998).

Yet another of the most beautiful of Lakeland villages which has been swamped by visitors in recent years is Hawkshead. The result has been an avoidance of the immediate area by those who enjoy a walk. This route restores the feel of the place by arriving there on foot, on the side opposite to the car park, and leaving across the fields from the churchyard. It is gentle countryside and gentle walking and, genuinely, one of the finest and most interesting of Lakeland's centres of population.

The Walk
Go towards the rear car park and, taking the gate beside the next cottage, enter the field by an iron kissing-gate. Turn half-right to a wooden kissing-gate in the far corner. Use a second gate and take the right-hand of two footpaths. To your left the view is now more open and takes in Wansfell and Froswick, on the two sides of the Troutbeck valley, beyond Windermere. Cross the field diagonally right on an old grassy track to the corner of a wood and enter the former oak and hazel coppice which is now grazed by sheep. At the far side an up and over stile puts you onto the lane to Colthouse. Go left between the buildings of Loanthwaite Farm and turn right on a footpath 50 yards beyond, which is signed to Hawkshead, beside the silage pit .

Follow the right-hand hedge as far as a kissing-gate. Go through and then bear left along the left-hand boundary beside a series of white-topped posts to meet the old track of Scar House Lane. Hawkshead village is now in view, backed by the outlying plantations of Grisedale Forest. Turn left for 50 yards, past pollarded oak and ash, and then go right on a footpath by a gate with an old flagstone fence, before you reach the barn. Continue over the marshy fields and follow the line of stiles with dog gates and cross the Black beck for the village

54

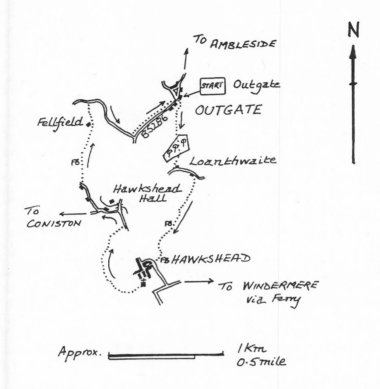

over a footbridge. Pass beside a black and white cottage with a wellingtonia, which has lost its top, in the garden. Walk between the cottages and the caravan site to the road.

Cross direct across the road and walk up Red Lion Yard and under the arch into Main Street. I suggest a zigzag route to take in the main features of this tiny town, but you will enjoy wandering through its narrow alleys whichever way you go. The building opposite the Red Lion has interesting decorative plasterwork above the doorway. Go to the right of this and turn left up the alleyway and right opposite 'Grandy Nook' at the end. Tucked round the corner is Anne Tyson's Cottage, where Wordsworth lodged while he attended the Grammar School (both Anne Tyson, and her lodgers, moved out to the hamlet of Colthouse part way through his years here). On the left, 10 yards beyond 'Hillfoot', is a narrow passage which takes you through to Flag Street over a beck. Once there, go left into the corner of the Market Place. There are several buildings of 15th century vintage. Keep to the left and make your way back into Main Street and go a little right to find the National Trust shop and the Beatrix Potter Gallery. On view are a selection of her superbly accurate wildlife paintings (the selection is changed from time to time) and the offices in which her solicitor husband, William Heelis, worked.

Continue by circling round the central block of buildings to return to the south-east corner of the Market Square and walk up in front of the Town Hall of 1790. Just beyond, turn to the left by the National Westminster bank and enter the churchyard of St Michael and All Angels. The floor is flagged and the construction oddly mixed. What you see is substantially the rebuilding of 1578, by Archbishop Sandys, but this was a chapel site long before that. From the church door, walk round the tower end and drop down to the left to find the delightful Old Grammar School of 1575; it was in use until 1909. This is now a museum and you will find that Wordsworth was not the only old boy to achieve fame. (It is open from Easter to October and on Sunday afternoons throughout the year.)

Your route now leads back up past the church to the footpath in the south-west corner and along the flagstone fence to a kissing-gate. Take the right-hand footpath for Coniston and Tarn Hows. The clear path joins a track and goes past the Vicarage. At a T-junction turn left and right before the entrance of Walker Ground to follow the footpath across the fields past an isolated Norway spruce to find a gate, half-hidden behind a sycamore and signed 'To Keen Ground only'. Use this and drop over the field to the right to join the access drive just below the house at an iron gate beyond the lime trees. Walk down the drive to the main road and go left and cross the bridge to the gate on the left to Hawkshead Hall Gatehouse. The key to this must be obtained from the National Trust shop in Hawkshead. The manor of Hawkshead was once the property of Furness Abbey and this was probably part of their grange, or farm. Return over the bridge and turn up the lane to the right. There is a good view of the rest of the remaining buildings of the Hall from across the beck.

Climb up the lane a little, taking care round the blind bend by the sawmill, and take the first right along Skinner How Lane. Turn right on a footpath just beyond the buildings at Violet Bank and cross the field to a kissing-gate and a flag footbridge over Thurs Gill beck and walk straight up to the stile by the gate on the brow. Swing half-right on a grassy track and pass close to the fairly modern house at Fellfield and use the access track to the road opposite Field Head. Go to the right round the cottage of Ben Fold. A glimpse of Esthwaite Water, beyond Hawkshead, can be had from this point, and to Gummers How beyond that. Continue along the lane. By the entrance to Field Head House is a Victorian post box let into the wall. At the T-junction with the main road, take the path on the inside of the wall on the left and follow it back to Outgate.

Haverthwaite
The Angler's Arms

About a decade ago the main road through the Backbarrow gorge was diverted, a new bridge over the river Leven was built, and Haverthwaite, especially the part in which the Angler's Arms stands, returned to relative peace. The former industrial nature of this area is no longer very obvious but it was the existence of a thirsty workforce which occasioned the building of the pub in the late 1700s. The result is a rather more imposing edifice than you might expect in an apparently rural setting. The inside is equally on the relatively grand scale.

From Monday to Saturday food is served from 11.45 am to 2 pm and from 6 pm to 9.30 pm (9 pm in the winter); on Sundays the hours are 12 noon to 2 pm and 7 pm to 9.30 pm (9 pm in the winter). The menu is an extensive one and is titled to keep up the angling theme. There are special children's and vegetarian menus, and a snack menu caters for the lighter eater. What is on offer is good, straightforward fare – and none the worse for being so. The busy trade evidences the success of such an approach with folk coming some distance for the grills, gammon and steaks.

Bar times in this freehouse are 11 am to 3 pm and 6 pm to 11 pm Monday to Saturday, and 12 noon to 3 pm and between 7 pm and 10.30 pm on Sundays. Theakston's ales are complemented by Tetley

Falstaff and dark mild, and Gillespie's Scottish stout. There is a more enterprising approach to wines than is common with a standard list of 14 and a landlord's private selection for the connoisseur. A pleasant terrace above the angle of the road does duty as a beer garden. Families are welcome as are well-controlled dogs in the bar. Accommodation is available.

Telephone: 015395 31216.

How to get there: Turn off the A590 from the short section of dual carriageway opposite the Lakeside and Haverthwaite Steam Railway.

Parking: There is extensive parking on the old road.

Length of the walk: 3 miles. Map: OS Landranger 97 Kendal and Morecambe (inn GR 348840).

The unhappy chance of the timing of the final closure of the Backbarrow Ironworks robbed us all of an industrial heritage which would have been a rival to Ironbridge. As it is, those who are prepared to walk, and to investigate a little, will find the wooded slopes around Haverthwaite and Backbarrow hide a great deal of interest. The walk is a pleasant one, in any case, but it does have a steepish climb for about ¹/₂ mile.

The Walk

Begin from the terrace of the Angler's Arms and go down the steps to the lane and along to the right around the bend; this needs a little care for oncoming traffic. At the row of cottages on the left, turn into the woodyard, find the path into the field behind the office hut and walk along the river bank to the bridge. Cross over the river Leven, take the first turn to the left and use the second entrance to enter the Low Wood complex of buildings. The remaining standing buildings are now devoted to a variety of craft enterprises – crystal glass, furniture, studios etc. The clock tower once housed offices, and the saltpetre and charcoal refineries. At the far side of the yard is the entrance to a caravan site which stands on the remains of the gunpowder works (and is private) – licensed in 1799 and operating until 1935. Leave the yard to the lane once more and go past the cottages. Follow the bridleway into the woods to the left. The track passes along the water leat of the works and the occasional remains of an old engine house, and other buildings, can be seen through the overgrowth. The route gently rises towards Low Brow Edge and there are excellent views of the whole of the gorge, the railway, and the Backbarrow buildings, over the field wall. At the lane to Bigland turn to the left down the footway.

Pass a playing field on the right and take the path left opposite Fellside.

58

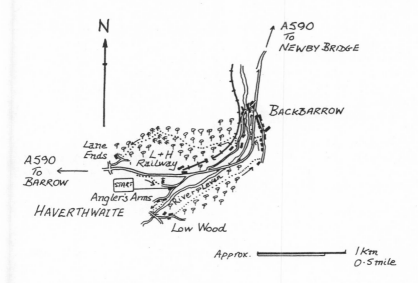

N

A590
To
NEWBY BRIDGE

BACKBARROW

Lane
Ends

A590
To
BARROW

L+H
Railway

START

Angler's Arms

HAVERTHWAITE

River Leven

Low Wood

Approx. ▭ 1 Km
0.5 mile

This descends quickly to a tunnel under the new road. Bear up to the right on the far side and come up to the road to pass the bottom of the Brow Foot lane on the right. A little beyond, turn down to the left and walk through to the road beside the White Water Hotel and the Timeshare complex. Cross to the far side of the bridge and look at the area from the corner of the lane which runs up-river. In medieval days there was a corn mill here which was converted to paper production. This burnt down in 1782 and the present two large mill buildings were put up for the spinning of cotton and flax. In the 1890s the manufacture of ultramarine blue began (a few will remember the bright stain of the powder on all the walls around) and lasted, with interruptions, until 1981. On the bridge abutment, well above the usual level of the hurling torrent, is a stone marking the flood level on 3rd November 1893; the rapid rise has already caught out the hotel bar on the downstream side of the bridge. It is down this river that some of the most difficult canoeing in England takes place. On the pool above the river weir, however, swans calmly sail.

Continue along the river with a leat on your left which leads to a pool and a turbine house: it is still in use and the hum of the blades can be heard. This is at the start of the site of the former Backbarrow Ironworks, operational from 1698 until 1967. Until well into this century the iron was smelted by charcoal. Initially this came from the surrounding woodlands of Furness and is one of the main reasons why so much woodland in the area has been coppiced. Much of the site was cleared when it closed but it is possible to see the base of the chimney, and some of the other buildings, over the wall on the left. Continue for about 200 yards and cross to a footpath up the bank to the right; keep right and go up to beside the railway. From this point you are looking down on the charcoal store for the ironworks which, latterly, was fed by a branch line. Cross over the line of what is now the Lakeside and Haverthwaite Railway and climb steadily, and fairly steeply up the bank into the woodland. In 100 yards you pass a stone building on the right which puzzlingly contains some sort of tank packed around with charcoal.

The path rises amongst conifers – spruce, larch, and western hemlock to begin with and then goes into old oak coppices at the top of the first rise. Down to the left, you can see the village school by the road. Gaps in the woods have been newly planted up. The whole area of Haverthwaite Heights is now a reserve in the care of the National Park Authority. Where the track swings right, continue ahead on a path which crosses a runnel and then drops several feet over a rock step. To the left is a boggy area with many alders. Further along the left-hand bank is almost pure wood of yew trees. The path meanders up and down and, at one point, actually crosses over an old charcoal burner's pitstead. This is recognisable by its flat, circular shape, about 15 ft in diameter, and the lusher growth of grasses on its surface. Eventually, you will reach a T-junction in a plantation of larch on the crest. Go left on the path, between old walls, and notice the remains of a stone hut to the right in the bracken; a woodsman's or charcoal burner's temporary home. The path drops between darker spruces and a view opens up the Rusland Valley to the right to Coniston Old Man. The bottom of the path is through broadleaved trees once more and exits to a lane opposite farm buildings at Lane Ends.

Go left and right, round the end of the buildings and down to the main road. Cross over with great care and walk left along the verge for about 300 yards to a gap in the wire fence to the right. The path leads to a stile over the wall. Turn to the left to the gate and walk along the old road to a second gate. Through this, and to the left, is the Victorian church of St Anne. The village is certainly over 1,000 years old, however, since its Norse name means 'the clearing where the oats were grown'. A few more yards will return you to the pub.

Within 150 yards of the pub door, across the main road, is the former Haverthwaite station site and the base for operations of the Lakeside and Haverthwaite Railway. The opportunity to look at this and, perhaps, to take a ride on a steam train up to Lakeside and on a lake steamer then, if you wish, should not be missed. The line opened in 1869 and closed to passengers in 1946. Goods traffic ceased when the ironworks closed. Re-opening as a steam enthusiasts' and tourist attraction was in 1973. Trains run at Easter and from May to October.

Flookborough
The Hope and Anchor

The link with the sea and the sands of Morecambe Bay is no longer so obvious as it used to be. Even the name of the place misleads: 'flukes', or locally caught small plaice, are not its origin but rather a Viking called Floki who came in from the sea in the tenth century. Reclamation of the low lying land by embankments around 1800 has moved the tides from Flookborough's doorsteps and only the few remaining signs saying 'Shrimps for sale' give an inkling of the past. The Hope and Anchor, just off the surprisingly large square, once served local fishermen rather than the passing tourist. It is but the successor to many an ale-house which has provided sustenance to this former market centre, first granted its charter by Edward I.

The menu here presents a choice of fairly standard meals at very reasonable prices. The snack eater, vegetarians and children are specially catered for. A good, plain soup of the day, followed by a gammon steak, and a choice from the sweets on the specials board would stand anyone in good stead for the bracing breezes off the Bay. Service is from 12 noon until 9 pm Mondays to Saturdays and from 12 noon until 3 pm and between 7 pm and 9 pm on Sundays.

This a Hartleys (Robinson's) house and the bar is open all day from

61

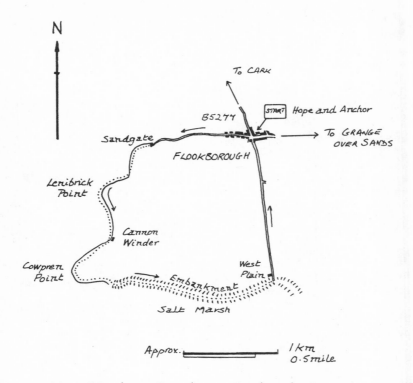

11 am to 11 pm Monday to Saturday; on Sundays the times are 12 noon to 3 pm and between 7 pm and 10.30 pm in the evening. The main beers are Hartleys XB and Robinson's best bitter, with stout, lager and cider on offer. A beer garden is situated to the rear and a children's play area is provided. Families are accommodated in the half-bar by the games room. Accommodation is available. Dogs are welcome.

Telephone: 015395 58733.

How to get there: Use the B5277 from the A590 via Grange over Sands, from the east, or via Haverthwaite and Cark, from the west.

Parking: Park in the main square a few yards from the pub.

Length of the walk: 4½ miles. Map: OS Landranger 97 Kendal and Morecambe (inn GR 367758).

Parts of the edge of Morecambe Bay are unique in south Cumbria for the land reclaimed from the sea, and for the few areas of arable farming in this part of the county. Flookborough's past, and a little of its present, link it with the sea and this walk's route provides an opportunity for a bracing stroll in the salt breezes with very easy, and usually, dry going underfoot.

The Walk

A few paces across Market Street, to the left of the pub door, old cottages are dated 1686 and there is an old cross, rebuilt in the late 1800s. From these walk across the square (which was, in fact, created by the demolition of a chapel and graveyard) and take the road to the west past The Corner Shop towards Sandgate. Rows of small terraced cottages include one dated 1637 BIA. Climb up the little brow, past the clematis of modern bungalows, until you can see the First World War crescent of Ravenstown, isolated amongst the fields. Ahead stretches the ridge of Low Furness across the estuary of the river Leven, where Chapel Island rides close to the Ulverston shore with the Hoad and its monument behind. Drop gently down towards the shore between cobbled walls and hedges of ash and thorn. The fields around wave with ripening grain crops in summer. Behind lies the estate around Holker Hall and the backdrop of Bigland Heights.

The farm at Sandgate sells vegetables from a barn shop and the sheep graze the salt-marsh on the far side of the yard. Walk through and turn along the track above the shore to the left. This is where travellers used to wait for the guides to show them the way across the dangerous sands. Ships fished the mussel beds here until the early years of the century when the estuary silted up too much. Down on the flats, shelduck, oystercatcher, lapwing and wading birds fussick for food. Cross the stone bridge with the tidal flood gate below and continue on the boulder beach below the eroding clay cliff of Lenibrick Point. There is a rough stile over the fence which runs out seaward and gorse and yellow creeping flowers decorate the sward to your left while green weed from the sea lies in pools to the right. At the 16th century farm of Cannon Winder (really 'canon', since the name derives from the monks of Cartmel Priory who once owned it) with its round chimney, small windows, and stone balls on top of the gateposts by the shore, continue past on the seaward side. Across the bay is Sea Wood, by Bardsea, and the Mausoleum on the hill to the right of it.

Sea campion and thrift grow almost amongst the roses at the top of the shore and the song of larks and linnets mixes with the cries of redshank from the sands of the Bay. At Cowpren Point the view swings round to Humphrey Head, with Arnside Knott beyond, and Morecambe, Heysham, and the Bowland Fells across the sands to their right. You may need to negotiate an electric fence at this point, but there should be plenty of driftwood to help hold it down while you stride over. Around

63

the Point the Old Embankment begins. Its sheltered inner ditch results in early blossoming of the thorn in the hedges and a boisterous growth of water crowfoot. Cows stand in the cooling water and quietly chew the cud. The gentle stroll along here gives time to speculate on the quirks of naming in our landscape. Until Whitaker suggested, in 1771, in his History of Manchester that the estuary named by Greek geographer Ptolemy in AD 150 could be the one we are walking beside, no one had thought to give it any special name at all, let alone 'Morecambe': the even more recent town is, of course, named from the Bay. At the end of the embankment the path joins the lane beside West Plain Farm and the entrance to Lakeland Leisure Park.

Go back towards the village along the wide verge. Pass the old Cark Airfield on the right where you can try parachuting, if you wish. A few wartime buildings remain and a lone hangar. A mini-industrial estate exists along the road with a garage and a place for car repairs. On the left is what is left of 'Flookborough Fishermen Ltd' which used to process locally caught shrimps and fish but finally closed when regulations for hygiene during preparation became too costly to meet. The ditches are the haunt of herons and contain masses of the tiny, floating fern Azolla while the fields echo to the sound of curlew. At the caravan site a lane runs to the right and passes the pele tower at Wraysholme, below the hill called Kirkhead. On the little hill to the half-right, beyond the village, local children rolled their 'pace eggs' at Eastertime as recently as the 1930s. Rise back into the village beside the barn conversion at Stockdale Farm and re-enter the square.

15 Bowland Bridge
The Hare and Hounds Country Inn

Bowland Bridge is a delightful hamlet of white-painted houses which sits on the old road from Kendal, guarding the crossing from Westmorland into Lancashire. The pub looks down the little brow to the bridge and has done for 400 years. The present landlord (an ex-Liverpool and England footballer – as the displayed trophies reveal) is justly proud of the old stones and beams of the cosy interior and aims for a warm welcome to all beside the open fires.

Food is available from 12 noon until 2 pm and, in the evenings, from 6.45 pm to 9 pm Monday to Friday and on Sunday, and between 6.30 pm and 9.30 pm on Saturdays. The usual light meals of sandwiches and salads are complemented by pizzas and main courses range from sausage to salmon. A rib-tickler, in Westmorland, and fine for a cold winter's day, is Giant Yorkshire Pudding filled with Cumberland sausage and onion gravy! The specials board will include a vegetarian dish of the day and is particularly famed for duck when it's available.

In this freehouse Tetley Traditional, Boddingtons and Greenalls keg beers are on draught. Labatt's and Carlsberg lagers, and stout, are joined by Gaymer's dry cider and Copperhead, a sweet one. Families are most welcome indeed, as are dogs on the lead. The forecourt is broad and open and has deservedly popular tables from which to watch the world go by. The bar is open all day from 11 am to 11 pm (10.30 pm on Sunday). A high standard of accommodation is available.

Telephone: 01539 568333.

How to get there: From the A5074 (Lyth Valley road) turn at the sign for Bowland Bridge at the top of the hill west of Crosthwaite. From the A590 turn north on the sign for Cartmel Fell in High Newton and follow through on the signs for Bowland Bridge.

Parking: A large car park is adjacent to the pub.

Length of the walk: 4¹/₂ miles. Map: OS Landranger 97 Kendal and Morecambe (inn GR 417895).

The upper part of the Winster valley is a land, par excellence, of the old 'statesman' farms. The walk passes three of these and includes some pleasant fields and woodlands. On the route there is also the fine old church of Cartmel Fell.

The Walk
Leave the pub in the direction of the bridge and turn to the left on the lane signed for Witherslack. In about ¹/₄ mile go right on the footpath through the gateway entrance to Burblethwaite Mill; in this case a former corn mill. Go across the bridge into the garden and immediately to the left by the lily pond and over the stile into a field. Follow a series of arrows and stiles through five fields until you are below the house at Pool Garth and a converted barn to its right. At this point, the path bears left between walls for 10 yards and then goes directly up the bank through a wall gap until you are just below the garden wall at Pool Garth. On the left you will find a small gate into the adjacent field. Use this and go to the left through the steel gate at the far left-hand corner. Bear round right to a second steel gate above a farm. Continue right on the track for 20 yards and turn up right into the churchyard of St Anthony's, Cartmel Fell.

This is a quite outstanding small church. Founded by the will of Anthony Knipe, of Burblethwaite Hall, in 1504, it enabled the inhabitants of this remote area to be christened, wedded, and be buried without having to go all the way to Cartmel Priory. The inside contains two fine box pews (with game boards carved in them, no doubt by idle hands), a three-decker pulpit, and interesting glass, which probably came from the Priory. The floor is flagged – though largely covered by carpet now – and slopes down to a hole in the corner through which the soiled rushes could be brushed out. The churchyard is a pleasant haven

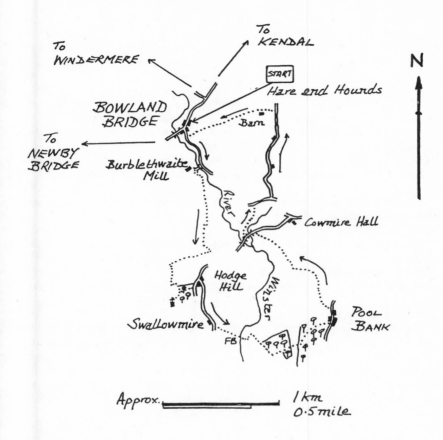

To KENDAL

To WINDERMERE

START

Hare and Hounds

BOWLAND BRIDGE

Barn

To NEWBY BRIDGE

Burblethwaite Mill

River

Cowmire Hall

N

Hodge Hill

Winster

Swallowmire

FB

Pool Bank

Approx. ⸻ 1 km
0·5 mile

of peace surrounded by trees. Immediately outside the lychgate is the former school converted into a village institute in the 1970s. Return to the lower entrance to the churchyard.

Cross over the track to a stile in the corner of the wood and go down the path amongst old coppice trees. Some of the coppice stools are as much as 12 ft across, the centres long having died away to leave a ring of stems; their age is certainly in the many hundreds of years. At the lane turn to the left and go down 70 yards to look up the yard outside Hodge Hill. Now a hotel, this is a former farm belonging to the Philipsons of Calgarth, by Troutbeck. The gallery above the doorway might, in this case, really have been used for spinning on warm summer evenings. Some of the smaller glass panes of the windows are still original blown glass and inside (not open to the casual visitor) are ancient carved cupboards and a doorway dated 1692.

Go now round the corner, between the barns, and along the lane for Grange over Sands. A wide view of Whitbarrow Scar and Yewbarrow opens out across the valley (see Walk 18). On the right you will pass an area of coppice woodland which is still being cut in rotation, about once every twelve to fifteen years. At the first farm on the right, called Swallowmire, take the footpath to the left and bear across the field just right of the obvious hollow; this gets extremely wet in winter. Reach the river Winster at a stile and footbridge and turn left and right on the far side, following the arrows. This takes you along the edge of a wood which you will eventually enter through a large gate. Go to the right on the track and then left in front of an open barn and through the old coppiced woodland to exit onto the lane just south of Pool Bank. The main farmhouse of this tiny hamlet juts out into the lane and has its door dated 1693 HIK (for the Hartleys). Again there is a gallery. Inside (not open to view) are old oak partition walls and an overmantel dated 1698. One of the other buildings carries the even older date of 1655 and all have drip stones standing out of the wall to shed the rain away from the footings and keep the inside dry.

Through the hamlet, and to the left, is a wooden fieldgate and a path. Bear to the right along the boundary. Across the valley Gummers How stands out on the ridge above Windermere and the long view is to the high fells of the central Lake District. The green track descends to a farm bridge over Copy beck. Across the field to the right is Cowmire Hall. It is hardly believable that, in 1964, this was threatened with submergence by a proposal for a reservoir! The Hall is built around a medieval pele tower, with walls four feet thick, which belonged to the Flemings. The resulting tall building is very plain and austere.

From the stile, continue between the stone gateposts and then bear right over a rocky knoll and then go half-left to where the hedge and wall meet. Use stone steps down into the next field and, at the far side, cross right of the old hedge and wall line to a stile right of the river bridges. Turn left and go over the first bridge (the next one is Lobby bridge, the old county boundary) and then right on a footpath up the Arndale beck. Edge a little left to the stile in the middle of the facing hedge and wall boundary and walk up the left-hand boundary of the next field, lined with damson trees, to a gate onto the lane. Turn right down the brow and then left in 200 yards on the lane past Woodside Farm on the right and then a white painted cottage on the left. About 250 yards past this there is a stile to the left and a path to the right of the stone barn, past a somewhat rubbish-filled pond, and across the rocky field to a large up and over stile. Continue direct across the fields to emerge onto the first lane you took, just behind the pub

16 Staveley
The Eagle and Child

Staveley, 'the place where the staves (of wood) were got', is still, today, a place where wood is an important raw material and the sturdy façade of the Eagle and Child overlooks the confluence of the two rivers which provided so much of the power for the wood-working machinery in the past. The name of the pub comes from the coat of arms of the Strickland family. Now there is a by-pass to the village, traffic no longer thunders within inches of the door but the pub has, if anything, profited from that and plies a goodly trade both locally and with visitors.

Food is available between 12 noon and 2 pm and from 6 pm to 9 pm in the evenings. The present landlords have expanded the menu considerably and there is a good range of light meals and more substantial fare. Out of the ordinary local specialities are a salad with Westmorland boiled ham, and a ploughman's lunch with smoked Westmorland cheese. Specials of the day may include a warming beef in beer, and fisherman's pie. There are special menus for both vegetarians and the children.

As a freehouse the bar times are currently 11 am to 3 pm and 6 pm to 11 pm (all day in the summer) and , on Sundays, 12 noon to 3 pm and 7 pm to 10.30 pm. Theakston's XB and best bitter are joined by

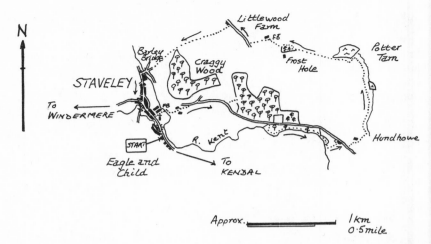

Tetley's best bitter, Guinness, lager, and Strongbow cider. The delightful beer garden is across the road on the bank of the rushing river Kent – where dippers, mergansers and kingfishers search for food for their own families; you are free to eat your own food here with a purchase of drinks. Dogs are not permitted.
Telephone: 01539 82132.

How to get there: Approach from the A591 over the level crossing at the south-eastern end of the village. The pub stands beside the river bridge.

Parking: A moderate amount of parking is available at the pub.

Length of the walk: 5 miles. The climb up to Potter Tarn can be avoided by returning from Staveley Park Farm via Barley bridge so reducing the length to only 1½ miles. Map: OS Landranger 97 Kendal and Morecambe (inn GR 472980).

Staveley has long been a centre for wood-using industry and the walk includes both past and modern examples. The circuit also visits three sites at which woodlands have been preserved for their landscape value, their wildlife, and their general amenity. The part of the route to and from Potter Tarn requires effort to negotiate steep slopes.

The Walk
Cross over the river bridge and over the road and go along the footway to the church tower on the right, standing alone in its former graveyard. This is all that remains of St Margaret's which began building in 1338;

the new church, at the far end of the village, replaced it in 1865. Staveley has always been, as Dorothy Wordsworth wrote in her Journal 'The first mountain village'. Staveley was the place chosen for the meeting, in January 1621, of local farmers who held their land by Border Tenure (by which they provided some of the defence against invading Scots) when they protested against the attempt by James I (and VI) to abolish it. Turn to the right on the path between the Duke William pub (which is about 600 years old) and the tower and go beside the works of Staveley Wood Turning, to a footbridge across the river Kent.

Leave the village behind now and bear to the right, along the field edge, to the yard of Staveley Park Farm. Go through the gates and between the house and the barn and up the brow along a deeply worn section of track to the lane. Turn to the right and walk along with Craggy Wood on the bank to the left. This is the first woodland of note within the Lake District National Park and very visible from the A590; as a consequence it is now in the care of the Park Authority. Continue past the lane up to the left and drop down to a fieldgate and stile on the left. Divert across the field to the small gate (not the stile) to Dorothy Farrer's Spring Wood reserve, belonging to the Cumbria Wildlife Trust. In recent years a coppice rotation has been re-established in this corner of woodland and there is an information board. Return to the lane and go left.

The lane borders old coppices on the left, with mayflowers, Jack by the hedge, and wood sorrel on the banks, and passes by a small sewage works. Just before a field on the left, go right into Beck Middle Ings wood, belonging to the Woodland Trust, and use the informal path down to the river bank. The path parallels the river downwards through old coppice with a wonderful show of wild flowers in spring and early summer. On the river bank are old alders which have, at some time, been laid as a hedge, and have now regrown into tall trees. At the far end emerge by a farm bridge over the river; the Dales Way passes by on the other bank. Turn away from it and go up the bank towards Hagg Foot Farm and walk to the left below the wall to regain the lane. Turn right and pass the buildings. Downstream, the buildings of the original Cropper's paper works of 1750, at Cowan Head, can be seen. In about 150 yards is an access lane to Hundhowe and an old sign for Mirefoot. Go up on the right-hand curve past the old farmhouse at Low Hundhowe and beside the barn to a gate onto the old road. At the top of the rise take the path to the left signed for Potter Tarn.

Gradually rise beside an old sunken track. There are fine views to the south over Kendal and to the Coniston fells in the west. A row of oaks marks the line of the old hedge. At a concrete hut with an iron fence round it, keep right and cross the Thirlmere pipeline and continue up the same side of the beck past tumbling waterfalls in a wooded ghyll. At a crude stone stile by the dam of Ghyll Pool pick up the green track to the left and emerge on to the open fell below the dam of Potter Tarn. Go to the up and over stile on the left. The view from here is magnificent. Pipits sing overhead as you now bear right of the knoll and cross short-cropped grass to pick up another green track by a stony bank and drop down steeply to a stile by a hogg (sheep) hole where three walls meet.

Continue steeply down to the track below and follow the signs through the gate ahead and past the larch plantation by the farm of Frost Hole. Follow the beck upwards and cross through the garden at Birk Field. Use the access track up to the lane and go right along to Littlewood Farm. Up the valley is the top of Ill Bell, on the far side of Kentmere. Turn left through the yard and follow the signs up the brow using a line of up and over stiles past the wood to the left. From the top the view opens out up the Kentmere valley. Pass coppice woodland on your left – this is the other side of Craggy Wood – and go very steeply down the right-hand boundary to exit to the lane by Barley Bridge Farm.

Go right and left over the bridge and walk in front of the works of Kentmere Papers, once a bobbin mill, and where they now make packaging and photographic paper. This latter part of the business was originally based on the use of diatomite from the bottom of Kentmere Tarn, which was used to put the smooth surface on the paper. In the past, the village has had corn, woollen, and also smelt mills. Just a few yards along the lane to the right by the memorial is the Victorian St James' church; it has a window by Burne Jones and William Morris. Use the footway to the village centre outside the house called The Abbey. Built in 1844 as a hotel it is now a residential home for the elderly. Round the bend of the road to the right is a cabinet-maker's craft shop, across the road, behind the toilets, is a wheelwright's and undertaker's and, standing in the corner of the garden on the far side of the river Gowan is a mill-grindstone from the paper-making works at Cowan Head: all wood-linked activities.

Turn to the left and walk about 100 yards to the entrance to Staveley Wood Turning Co. The former coppice storage barn, with its characteristic round pillars, has been converted into a mini-industrial estate by filling in between the pillars. Access is public, so do walk in to have a look; a surprise is the existence of a French bakery which will happily sell you patisseries for your tea! Across the road, behind the butcher's, is a most unusual theatre, The Round House, which is so shaped because it is inside the base of the former gas holder of the 'Staveley near Kendal Gas Company'. Return to the road and go left to reach the start once more.

17 Crook
The Sun Inn

Square on to the road from Kendal to Bowness and the Windermere ferry, the Sun Inn presents a fine, unpretentious whitewashed face to the passing world. The ferry has plied the lake for nigh on 1,000 years so the pub, at 1683, is a youngster by comparison. The interior is as simple and as uncomplicated as the exterior with an excellent atmosphere of welcome.

Meals are served between 12 noon and 2.30 pm and from 6 pm (7 pm on Sundays) and 9.30 pm. Sandwiches and filled jacket potatoes make a suitable light meal for the not-so-peckish while a good choice of main meals will set you up for the rest of the day. Time after time, the pub which makes the minor interesting change to standard meals is the one which attracts the custom, and the Sun is no exception. Ham and eggs is common enough, but who else bothers to include the fried bread like mother used to do? The children and vegetarians are catered for too.

The Sun is a freehouse and carries the full range of Theakston's beers, Boddingtons bitter and Youngers mild. Lagers include McEwan's, Beck's and Coors. Guinness stout, and Woodpecker and Strongbow ciders are on draught. Wines are also available. The bar is open all day from 11 am to 11 pm Monday to Saturday and from 11 am to 3 pm and between

7 pm and 10.30 pm on Sundays. An area is kept for non-smokers and families are especially welcome. A small area by the road gives scope for some outside tables where you can sit in the sun. Dogs are not permitted inside during food service hours.

Telephone: 01539 821351.

How to get there: Take the B5284 from the A592 south of Bowness or from the northern roundabout (Plumgarths) of the Kendal by-pass on the A590.

Parking: The main car park is at the end of the terrace of cottages adjacent to the pub.

Length of the walk: 4³/₄ miles. The short route (marked S on the sketch map) is 2¹/₂ miles. Map: OS Landranger 97 Kendal and Morecambe (inn GR 464951).

This pleasant circuit through quiet countryside wanders up and down with many a stile and gate. Sections are apt to be a bit wet underfoot. Several old farms and the former church of St Catherine are of historic interest.

The Walk

Turn to the right from the pub door and have a look at the restored 17th century village pinfold (where stray animals were kept) beside the small front car park. Use the footway to the corner of the lane by Sunny Point cottages. There is a fine view down the Winster valley to the left from here. Continue past into the dip, below the old mill dam, and next to the overspill channel, and climb up a short way until opposite the tall wellingtonia in the garden on the left. Turn right on the footpath by the second gate, signed to Beckside, and go ahead amongst the head-high gorse, broom and bramble beside the remains of the right-hand boundary wall. Emerge into a more open field on top of the bank and go forward over the stone bridge to the stile in the wall opposite Beckside beside the bridge. Go to the left past the barns and into the field and cross the stream to the second gate and stile on the right and move up the far side of the wall to an up-and-over stile.

For the shortened route do not use the stile but bear left and go over two stiles to come to the main road. Cross over almost direct and take the gate to a track in the field. At the corner of the wall keep beside it and up the brow to the tower of Old St Catherine's church, where the main route joins.

For the main route, use the stile to the right of the wall and continue upwards to a further up-and-over stile and ahead to the green track. Turn

74

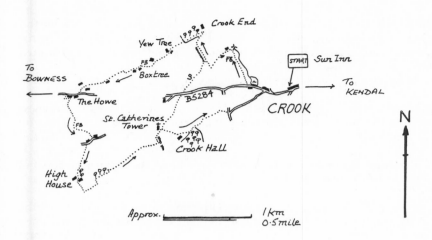

to the right. The view east is to Cunswick Scar and Scout Scar, above Kendal and down, southwards, to Whitbarrow Scar. Before reaching the house, use the kissing-gate to the left of the corrugated barn. Keep beside the left-hand boundary with the remains of an oak wood on your right, to an up-and-over stile at the top of the bank amongst gorse and broom. The view is even wider from here and includes Clougha Pike and Ward's Stone, behind Lancaster. Turn to the left through the yard at Yew Tree and go right at the kissing-gate at the end of the buildings and follow the fence across the field to an up and over stile and join the access track to the right towards Field Tenement.

On the hill to the right is the Monument, a look-out point for Scots raiders and used by the Home Guard in the last war. Before entering the yard, use the iron gate to the left and follow the right-hand boundary around the garden wall and drop across the field to a footbridge and go up to the yard of Box Tree. Keep to the right of the far barn, by a stone gatepost, and find a stile through the hedge on the right. Hold to the left-hand boundary wall as far as the gateway ahead and then go right up the wall and left at a corner in 30 yards to continue on the same line as before. From the stone stile by a telegraph pole, go ahead past the house at Sunny Brow and swing right on the grassy track to a stile with the amazing number of six steps to it. Follow the arrow through the gate to the left and go to the right to a kissing-gate onto the access to Birksey Brow, the grey house up to your right. Fifty yards to the left brings you to the main road.

Walk along to the right with some care and cross over to the left-hand verge before the blind bend. Pass the entrance to The Howe and the post-box in the wall by the farm entrance and find a stile over the wall to the left in 20 yards. Bear left under the big ash tree and follow the right of way through the farmyard and turn to the right. Bear slightly to the left down a track and then across three fields to a stone footbridge and stile onto another track. Turn to the left and walk up to the lane at Milldam past the old dam itself. Reputedly, there were almost 40 small mills within the parish at one time or another. Go right now, up the little brow, to the old farmhouse at Brow Head with its decorative plough, harrow, and flower garden. Pass this and take the first fieldgate to the left and bear half-right between scattered trees to a small gate in the corner of a fence and continue the line to a stone stile below an ash tree and cross the next field to another small gate at the top left. Do not go through the gate but use the stone stile to its right and follow the left-hand wall along the outside of the wood and into the yard of High House.

Exit to the right and find two stiles just beyond the end of the barn which take you through the chicken run beneath sheltering sycamores. Bear slightly to the right over the rocky brow and drop to a small gate in the wall and go left to the gate on the track. Follow this through a dog leg to cross the shelterbelt and find a cattle grid. Immediately, turn to the right on an old bridleway. Ignore the footpath sign to the right and continue straight ahead to drop down to a gate by trees in the dip. Walk up the left-hand boundary by the hedge and join a well-grooved track to the gap in the wall. Do not go through but turn left along the wall and find a squeeze stile in the corner and cross to the tower of Old St Catherine's church. This dates from the early 1500s but the church had become unsafe and was demolished and replaced by the new one, on the turnpike road, at the corner of Back lane to the north-west in 1887. This is where the short route rejoins the main one.

Turn to the east from the tower and use the gate onto a track which leads towards Crook Hall Farm. Walk to the left and go left into the field, away from the yard, and bear up to the right to the far corner of the trees. Use the stile here and continue along to the end of the wall and then bear up half-right and over the rocky knoll to an up-and-over-stile at the wall beyond. This is wheatear country and the perky birds flit from rock to wall and chatter at you as you pass. On the far side, go to the right of the rocky scar with the trees on it and down a dry valley to a kissing-gate at the left-hand corner. Drop down through a boggy patch amongst gorse and bracken to a stone stile onto the lane. Go immediately right and left and down Dobby Lane – a dobby (or dobbie) is a local form of sprite with something of a mischievous habit. The workshops of the former mill have been converted into dwellings and the old Mill Cottages refurbished most pleasantly; the mill itself has been demolished. Climb up briefly to the main road and cross to return right to the pub.

18 Witherslack
The Derby Arms

The Derby Arms used to be beside the main road west to Barrow and beyond but was by-passed by the new dual carriageway about a decade ago. The result is a much pleasanter venue to stop at to slake your thirst and fill that nagging corner. At a guess, its pillared porticoes indicate a mid-19th century building, but no date is visible. The inside is as warm and welcoming in winter and as cool and pleasant in summer as it was when it served the coaches passing this way.

The Derby makes rather a speciality of its pies with shortcrust pastry; steak and chicken and mushroom are excellent hot fillers in the old tradition. Lighter eaters are not neglected with salads, 'butties', and a variety of baked potatoes on offer. The vegetarians have a somewhat better choice here than at many pubs, as do the children. Serving times are from 12 noon until 2 pm and between 6.30 pm and 9 pm (except for Monday and Tuesday evenings in the winter).

This is a Vaux pub and has their Samson, light and mild on draught as well as Wards best bitter. Labatt's and Carlsberg lagers, stout, and Symonds Scrumpy Jack cider complete the range. There is an excellent beer garden at the side with a play area for the children. You are welcome to eat your own food outside with a purchase of drinks.

Dogs are welcome except in the tap room and dining room. There is usually a live music performance on Thursday evenings.
Telephone: 015395 52207.

How to get there: Witherslack is signed near the eastern end of the section of dual carriageway of the A590 west of the A5074 turn-off between Levens and Grange over Sands. The pub is on the crossroads almost immediately after the cattle grid.

Parking: A large car park is adjacent to the pub and there is plenty of space along the old road also.

Length of the walk: 5 miles. Map: OS Landranger 97 Kendal and Morecambe (inn GR 441830).

The walk goes through one of the most delightful small nature reserves in the county and passes by two others. The country is a mixture of woodland and open grazing, limestone and shaly gritstones and is generally rich in wildlife. As a walk it is very gentle, excepting only one short section, and usually dry underfoot.

The Walk

Leave the pub door along the old road to the left and pass the old lay-by, now used for road repair materials. At the bend, a bridleway strikes off to the right through a gate. Immediately, you are in the Latterbarrow Reserve of the Cumbria Wildlife Trust. Its ten acres hold more than 200 species of flowering plant and fern on the thin soils, and rock outcrops here and there. Scattered throughout are specimens of the Lancaster Whitebeam. Butterflies are common with the yellow brimstone in spring and the high brown and pearl bordered fritillaries later in the year; in high summer northern brown argus and the grayling may be seen. Birds include the spotted flycatcher.

The route follows the bridleway to the right and through the limestone grassland to a gate at the far end. Follow a worn path to a crossing of footpaths. Continue ahead and rise up slightly into a field and cross, towards the buildings at High Fell End. The barn to the right has been recently renovated but that beyond the old farm house is an original bank barn, with access from the lane behind. The farmhouse itself has old round chimneys.

Walk round the blind bend to the left for 100 yards and take the path which goes up to the right, signed to Witherslack Hall. This rises gently through coppice woods with the occasional beech, Scots pine, and yew. Eventually you reach a junction at a small cairn with a path going steeply down to the left. Take the right-hand fork and continue, more steeply up

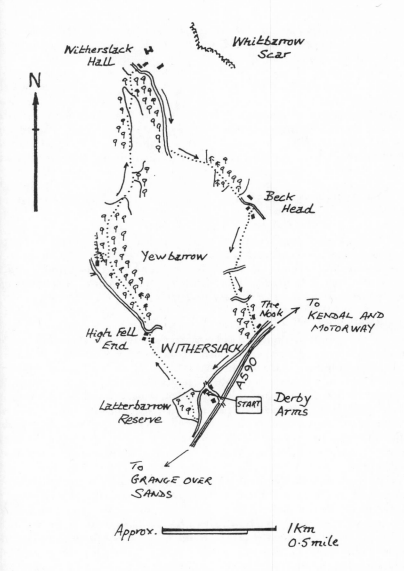

N

Witherslack Hall

Whitbarrow Scar

Beck Head

Yewbarrow

The Nook

To KENDAL AND MOTORWAY

High Fell End

WITHERSLACK

A590

Latterbarrow Reserve

START

Derby Arms

To GRANGE OVER SANDS

Approx. 1 Km
0.5 mile

for a while, until the path flattens off and an informal path is seen on the left. A few paces through the coppice hazel brings you out onto an open and airy grass platform on the top of a cliff with a fine view across the lower Winster valley to Cartmel Fell and Gummers How. Immediately down below is the parish church of St Paul's. This was built in 1669, as a result of the bequest of the Barwick brothers who were natives of this place. One became Dean of St Paul's in London, after an amazing career as a double-agent during the Civil War.

Return to the main path and continue through scrub birch and juniper to a gate onto the open grazed area of Yewbarrow. An obvious track crosses through a few scattered trees towards the wall of a wood. Whitbarrow Scar is clearly visible across the valley. The top of this is another Wildlife Trust reserve for its limestone pavements and rare plants, and the cliffs and woodland below are a reserve looked after by the National Park Authority. Follow the track through more woodland and past fields and a further wood to a grassy area, surrounded by the woods, called The Launds. Take the mossy walled track and bend right to come in view of Witherslack Hall Farm. Follow the lane around the bend to the right. On the bend is the entrance to Witherslack Hall – once a summer residence of the Earls of Derby and now a school – and a lane down to the old kennels. Climbing takes place on the cliffs but is restricted because of nesting peregrine falcons; ravens also nest here and within a couple of miles of this spot there may be as many as 50 badger setts. Return to the lane and continue down the valley. A bridleway is signed left to Beck Head. Follow this across the valley bottom and rise up slightly beside some large Scots pine and larch.

The track now descends gently through the wood and comes out into the open again beside a renovated barn on the right and joins a metalled lane. Keep directly ahead and go round the bend past the cottages to suddenly come upon the rising of the beck from the base of small cliff below a farm.

Walk towards the low bridge but turn hard right, into the yard before it (there is no sign), and pass between the house and the small breeze-block hut to a gate hidden behind. You now pass onto slates and grits and the vegetation immediately changes to gorse, bracken and brambles. Towards the far side a path crosses over from left to right but go ahead and find a stile and steps down to the lane in 10 yards. Go right for 50 yards and use the paired (oddly?) stile on the left signed to Rocky Common.

The path runs between low ridges of rock and drops down to an alder coppice in wet bottom land. On the bank to the left are crab apple trees. At a kissing-gate enter a lane and go to the left and to the top of the bend to a bridleway to the right. Use the bridleway past a house and over a brow to go by the door of The Nook and reach the old road. Go to the right and pass by hedges with blackcurrant, gooseberry, and spindle trees in them, to the crossroads beside the pub.

19 Sandside
The Ship Inn

The view across the estuary of the river Kent to the mountains of Cumbria and the limestone scar of Whitbarrow in the foreground is, without doubt, one of the finest in Britain. The Ship no longer has boats of any size plying past its door, as it did in the days of its youth around 1700, but it does have many a dedicated angler with rod and line at high tide patiently leaning on the rails along the road. At low tides, folk still 'tread' with their feet for flat fish hidden in the sand. Originally a coaching inn, it serves an extensive passing trade and has the additional adventure of the road nearby being flooded yet at very high tides.

A fitting starter, in keeping with the fishy location, is roll-mop herrings, which might be followed by ham and peaches (a pleasant change from pineapple), and one of the large selection of sweets which is chalked up daily. Several possibilities meet the needs of the vegetarian and even the children's menu has a vegetarian dish included. Food is available between 12 noon and 2 pm and from 6.30 pm to 8.30 pm Monday to Saturday, and from 12 noon until 2.30 pm and 7 pm to 8.30 pm on Sundays.

Summer opening of the bar is all day from 11 am to 11 pm but hours are reduced in the winter to 11 am to 3 pm and 6 pm to 11 pm (7 pm to

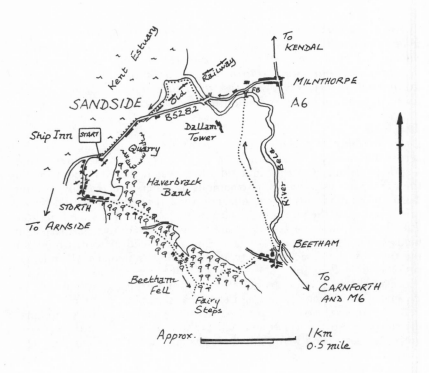

10.30 pm) on Sundays. This is a Scottish and Newcastle house (Pennine Inns) and carries their own beers, including McEwan 70/-, as well as Theakston best bitter. Lagers are McEwan's, Beck's and Coors, stouts are Guinness and Gillespie's, and the range is completed with Strongbow cider. Wine is available. Families are welcome, except in the public bar, and there is both a large beer garden and a garden play area for the children. Only guide dogs are permitted on the premises.

Telephone 015395 63113.

How to get there: From the centre of Milnthorpe on the A6 take the B6282 towards Arnside.

Parking: Permission to use the pub car park is not usually granted but adequate road side parking exists along the road in the Arnside direction.

Length of the walk: 5 miles. Map: OS Landranger 97 Kendal and Morecambe (inn GR 477817).

This is a walk of fine contrasts. Along the estuary the views are superb whilst the woods are dark, secret, and full of hidden flowers. Beetham village has been the centre of the district for 1,000 years and has a beautiful and interesting church as well as a couple of museums of exceptional quality. There are two short diversions of interest – to the Fairy Steps and into the village of Milnthorpe.

The Walk

Leave the Ship in the direction of Arnside and enjoy the view north across the estuary awhile and, at the right time of tide, vicariously enjoy a spot of fishing. On the right tide, too, watch the Kent bore race up the narrowing estuary – not so famous as others, but equally exciting! Turn up the road into Storth village to the left and cross the old railway bridge and pass the village hall. Turn left again into Yans Lane and take a further left, more or less opposite the post office, to pass the playing fields and continue ahead to what seems a dead-end. A footpath leads to the right by the garage opposite a cottage and is signed to Beetham. It runs beside a field for a short way and then plunges into Haverbrack Woods. The path wanders across rocky outcrops amongst hazel, ash, sycamore, beech, holly, yew and the occasional alien conifer.

At the top of the bank bear to the right on the broader track and ignore the subsidiary paths to left and right. Ultimately, drop a little to emerge onto a lane at a bend with a small car parking area (there is no sign here). Take the lane to the right as far as a gate to the left with a Dallam Tower Estate notice on it.

Walk along the good track surface between old coppices and scrubby pines. Much of the woodland grows on limestone pavements. Cross a ride with telephone cables running along it and come out into an open, grassy area on the summit of Beetham Fell, with eyebright, harebells, and hawkweed adding flashes of contrasting colour amongst the green. A finger post directs you to the minor diversion to Fairy Steps – a stone staircase up a narrow groove in a small limestone cliff. Return to the sign and continue on the track to the left (not signed) and take the path which turns half-left at the edge of the wood and drops by a wall with flat camstones to a stile and steps. Go down beneath beech trees on a clear path and at the crossing of the paths go left on the sign for Beetham. A broad track now descends gently through the woods. Several paths lead off to the left and any will lead you to a stile and a path across a field to exit onto the lane opposite the cemetery at the edge of Beetham village. Turn to the right and walk along to the church of St Michael.

Enter the churchyard by the gate next to the medieval Parsonage Farm. The tower, and other parts of the building, are 11th century and inside are glass and monuments of the 15th century. Leave the church under the lovely pergola of roses and go back onto the lane by a pair of Georgian houses on the opposite corner to the Wheatsheaf Hotel. Turn down the rise to the left and take the access road left just before the main A6 which is signed for Heron Corn Mill and the Paper Museum. Both are open daily from Easter to the end of October, except for Mondays. The mill site has been functional since at least 1096 and, for three and half centuries, belonged to St Mary's Abbey, at York. The Paper Museum relates to the paper works of Henry Cooke Ltd, which stands on the far bank of the river Bela.

Leave the museums from the north-west corner of the car park on a footpath, signed to Milnthorpe, up the field. There is a short, sharp climb up a new avenue of trees to an up-and-over stile and stone bridge beside large oaks and sycamores on the brow. Leave the river to the right and bear to the left of the hill ahead (which has an earthwork on the top, and a barn at the base) and contour round it through the park of Dallam Tower. The path runs in clear sight of the house. This dates from about 1720, with additions of 1826. It is not open to public view. A herd of fallow deer graze the park and you will surely come upon them, and accompanying sheep, as you continue on a line towards the edge of Milnthorpe village and the obvious black roof of a large barn.

The path crosses the river on a substantial stone bridge and exits to the main road by a large iron kissing-gate. Turn right for a diversion into Milnthorpe. The Market Place has an 18th century cross. Harmony Hall is about 1795, the old Workhouse is early 19th century and the Kitching Almshouses are of 1881. The tower on the hill, to the north, was reputedly built as a summer house.

Return to the edge of the village and continue along the B5282; there are further views of Dallam Tower as you walk along. Use the footway past Parkside and take care over the river bridge on the bend. Turn immediately right on a footpath signed for Sandside. Walk along the bank of the Bela, with the embankment of the old railway obvious on the far side. Where the Bela meets the Kent the view over the salt marshes is up the Lyth valley and the spire of Levens church should be clear on the right slope. Gulls, wildfowl and waders feed along the shore. A short stretch of limestone outcrops just round the bend and a ramp leads you up onto the bed of the old railway. Continue along this to some steps which lead up to the main road once more. Go right and make your way to the café car park at the corner. When the tide is out, it is possible to walk amongst the sea asters along the top of the shore back to the pub. Otherwise you must use the road with great care for oncoming traffic, for it is narrow between walls. On the way you pass Crown Cottage of 1728 and the intense contrast of the modern flats just beyond

Oxenholme
The Station Inn

At the northern end of the village of Oxenholme, the white-walled Station Inn stands at the point where the old road between Kendal and Kirkby Lonsdale crosses the route along the ridge. The building betrays its farm origins but the name misleads for this was the coach stop at the top of the hill before the days of the railway and it is not named after the upstart railway station which is, for so many, the point of change to the branch line into the heart of the Lake District.

Meals are served in the warm and welcoming bar room between noon and 2 pm and from 6 pm to 8.30. The range of the menu is considerable and attracts a strong local patronage to its home-cooked dishes. The meat choice covers the gamut of British fare and, nonetheless, manages a degree of originality. Neither vegetarians nor the children are forgotten – they have their own menu – and the specials (like game pie) and desserts of the day extend the possibilities even more. A pleasurable development, as a result of modern kitchen facilities, has been the better choice of worthwhile snacks on offer in many pubs. The jacket potato is a strong competitor with the time-honoured sandwich for many walkers and my experience here of one filled with chilli con carne left me well satisfied.

Drinking hours are from 11 am to 3 pm on weekdays, all day (11 am to

11 pm) on Saturday and from 12 noon to 3 pm and 7 pm to 10.30 pm on Sundays. The selection of real ales includes Theakston's, Boddingtons, and Flowers together with a guest beer which is changed monthly. Two lagers and two stouts on draught are joined by chilled wine by the glass or bottle. A row of classic malt whiskies tempts from the shelves behind the bar. In fine weather there is a pleasant beer garden to sit out in and an adjacent play area for children. Dogs are more than welcome here. Accommodation is available.

Telephone: 01539 724094.

How to get there: Approach from the A65 on the B6254 on the south-east edge of Kendal following the signs for Oxenholme and the station or use the B6254 from Kirkby Lonsdale.

Parking: You may park at the pub, or in a lay-by behind it on Hayclose Lane, or across the road beside the unfenced lane beyond the cattle grid.

Length of the walk: 5 miles. Map OS Landranger Sheet 97 Kendal and Morecambe (inn GR 536900).

The eastern ridge of the valley in which the town of Kendal lies is well known to locals but sadly neglected by off-comers. The views in all directions from The Helm are outstanding on a clear day and the reasons why main routes have followed this part of the valley of the river Kent throughout the centuries become very obvious indeed, and why it has thus always been an important site to defend. The second part of the route lies hidden amongst the steep-sided smooth hillocks, left behind by melting ice sheets more than 12,000 years ago, to the east between the Kent and the valley of the Lune.

The Walk

Cross the road slightly to the right from the door of the pub and go over the cattle grid onto the unfenced lane which runs south, along the western slope of The Helm, eventually crossing the A65 and dropping into Natland village. You have now entered common land which forms a finger of Natland parish stretching along this side of The Helm and lies open for all to take their exercise. Climb gently up the clear grassy path to the left to the crest and follow the wall along southwards to the highest point (only 400 ft) at the trig point at the far end.

It is worth stopping several times in this short distance to look at the views both far and near. Beyond Helsington Barrows and Kendal Fell, on the far side of the valley, rise the high tops from Coniston Old Man round to the Langdale Pikes; north-west lie Fairfield, Red Screes and the

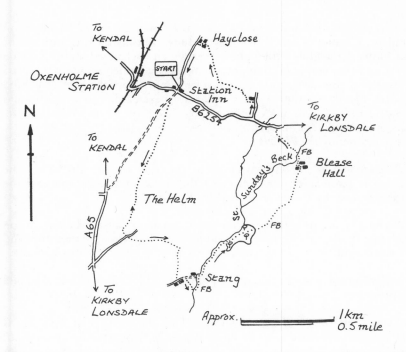

fells around the head of Kentmere; north-east are the rounded shoulders
of the Shap Fells – all these in the Lake District National Park. Due east
lie the Howgill Fells and the Pennines of the Yorkshire Dales National
Park; to the south are the hills of the Forest of Bowland and the nearer
limestone knolls of the country around Arnside and Silverdale. Almost
beneath your feet is the old woollen centre of Kendal with six fortified
sites within a bow shot of its river crossings; from prehistory, through
Roman, to medieval. Not much is left of most but the hill fort in which
you stand, on the top of The Helm, has very clear ditches and banks to
supplement the natural small crags on west and south. Across the valley,
in woods, beyond the tower of Natland church is a seventh site, Sizergh
Castle (a National Trust property) and an eighth is but 1 mile south of it
at Levens Hall.

A short, but steep drop off the end of The Helm takes you down to a
bridleway by the wall and a gate through to the left and, in a few yards,
to a lane along the bottom of the eastern slope of the hill. Cross directly
onto a farm access of parallel concrete tracks (there is no sign) and walk
down among daffodils, bluebells, celandine, and flowering cherry, with
singing wrens and warblers in season, to the first bend and bear off ahead
through an iron gate. Move slightly left across the field to a further gate

in a wall just below the outlet of a small tarn with coot, lapwing and black-headed gulls. The view ahead is of the rolling, smooth whale-backs of a whole field of mounds, left by the ice.

Stride across the outflow stream and pass through the gap in the wall at the corner on the left and immediately turn right up the hedge past an unusual tall, two-stemmed holly tree. At the far end, turn to the right through the gap and make for the iron gate in the corner. Bear across the next field, between the fence and the pond to your right, to reach a gate into a lane opposite a house called Foxfield and turn left to cross a cattle grid. Immediately bear to the right to reach a footbridge over St Sunday beck and cross to the far bank.

Turn to the left along the river bank and pass the old farm of Stang on the west bank. Alder, ash, sycamore, hazel, and both kinds of thorn line the banks of the water and the small islands of the beck. In spring, sunlight dapples the swathes of flowers beneath them. The path bears away from the river as you enter Blease Hall Wood. Exit from the wood by a kissing-gate and cross to an up-and-over stile and footbridge ahead. Follow the right-hand boundary and take the left of the two gateways at the field end to continue up by a ditch on your right. At the far gate pass through and now continue with the left-hand hedge, past a round water trough, to a green lane which leads you to the yard of the farm at Blease Hall. The old house within the group dates from 1600 and is said to have some of the finest plaster work in Westmorland but it is not open to view. Go straight through towards the converted barn and turn left between it and the smaller house on the brow to your left and find the gate into the field on the right. Drop down to the right again and through a gate before bearing left towards a footbridge across the beck. The path climbs, rather steeply, straight up the bank for a short distance and follows the right-hand hedge down towards the lane leading to the large farm at Strickley below. Just before reaching the far hedge, turn to the right through the last gap and make immediately across to the gate onto the B6254 just east of the entrance to Strickley.

Walk left, towards Kendal, along the verge, to cross the bridge over the beck and go right up Beehive Lane as far as the first farm entrance on the left 200 yards along. There is no sign here, but a bridleway runs in front of the house to the gate and then up the field to a second gate at the top left-hand corner. Go through and follow the wire fence on the left as far as the start of a wall at three gates. Here a track bears off right, about 20 yards short of a fast-flowing spring. Take the track and follow it up a broad, dry valley to the yard of Hayclose and use the entrance track onto the lane (again there is no sign). Turn left and walk along the verge to return to the pub.

Barbon
21 The Barbon Inn

Barbon lies under the eastern slopes of the delightful middle reaches of the valley of the river Lune. The 16th century Barbon Inn is in the upper part of the village with its range of buildings at right angles to the road. The original cottage atmosphere is retained beneath its black oak beams with open fires and high-back wooden settles on which to sit. It was 'upgraded' when the railway came by in the mid-19th century and has totally escaped the misguided efforts of the 20th.

The bar food menu is a wider one than many, with several local touches. The speciality here is, however, the set menu which is very highly rated indeed. The problem, as always, is to convey the quality and standard in but a few words. Perhaps suggesting a starter of home made chicken liver pâté followed by roast supreme of Lunesdale duck with a black cherry and apple sauce conveys something of your choice? Food service is from 12 noon to 2 pm and from 7 pm to 9 pm in the evening.

Theakston Old Peculier and best bitter are joined by Youngers Scotch ale, Murphy's stout, and Carlsberg lager on draught. Bar times are from 12 noon to 3 pm and 6.30 pm to 11 pm (7 pm to 10.30 pm on Sundays) Monday to Saturday. An attractive beer garden adjoins the rear of the pub and you are welcome to eat your own food here with a purchase of drinks. Families are welcome as are well-behaved dogs. Accommodation is available.

Telephone: 015242 7623.

How to get there: Take the A683 from Sedbergh or Kirkby Lonsdale and turn on the signs for Barbon, crossing the line of the old Roman road as you do so. The pub is on the Dent road at the top of the village, on the right just before the church.

*Parking:*Car parking is limited beside the pub but there should be no difficulty in finding a space beside the road. Alternatives exist in Barbondale (GR 657827) and at the end of the lane to Bull Pot (GR 663814) if you care to visit the pub part way round the circuit.

Length of the walk: 7½ miles. It is possible to shorten the route by returning down the Barbondale lane; 3⅓ miles. Map: OS Landranger 97 Kendal and Morecambe and 98 Wensleydale and Wharfedale (inn GR 629824).

Despite its length and the height reached, when taken in the direction suggested, this is not a difficult walk; a retreat down the valley road is the only way to shorten it. To do so is to miss one of the very finest of viewpoints in the whole county. There is plenty of contrast, too, between the Barbondale woods, the open fell, and the pastures of the Vale of Lune. Bird life and wild fruits of the wayside are both abundant.

The Walk

Turn up the valley from the pub and go along the village street. Only a few steps along is the church of St Bartholomew which replaced a chapel of the early 1600s in 1893. The tower is unusually a little wider than the nave and transept. Several of the internal furnishings were locally made. Go to the left, beyond the churchyard, and follow the sign along a lane to Barbon Manor. Cross the beck on a bridge with red sandstone copings and a fine grouping of five birch trees beside it. Zigzag up the access road to a footpath to the right.

Barbon Manor, of 1863, is in the Italian style but not open to the public. As you pass through the gate, take a glance at the view of the village and Lune valley behind. The route contours gently up the valley amongst woods beside the Barbon beck. There is a great variety of native trees and patches of spruce and larch provide contrast. Bird life is abundant with foraging tits, wrens, robins, blackbirds, and the occasional crazy cackle of a green woodpecker echoes amongst the trees above the splashing of the beck. By a bridge there is a delightful waterfall.

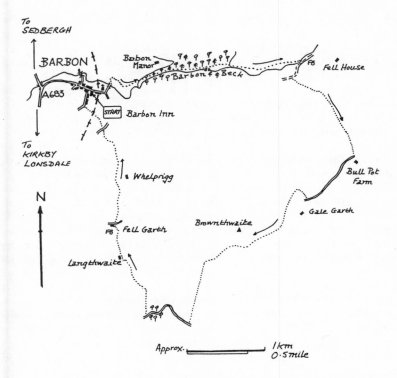

At the stone bridge, continue ahead on the track to an up-and-over stile by a gate (not up the track to the left). The track is now in open oak woodland, with scattered old birch and alder by the beck. The great grassy sweep of Barbon Low Fell is to the right, the High Fell is ahead, and an old lime kiln teeters on the bank of Castle Knott, up to the left.

Go through the iron gate by the sheep folds and use the ford or the nearby footbridge to cross to the road below the trekking centre at Fell House. Turn back along the lane towards the village and walk round the bend and over the bridge across Aygill and continue 50 yards to the second track to the left, which is signed as a bridleway to Bull Pot.

The only opportunity for a shortened walk is to return from this point along the road down the valley.

The track climbs steadily up the valley of Aygill, with several waterfalls almost hidden out of sight in little ravines. Come round the shoulder of the fell through bracken and bent grasses along the peaty, wet track. Over to the left are the ruins of mine buildings in Little Aygill, and the mounds of old coal pits dot the moor half-left. Pipits sing above while wheatears dart along the walls and the crows wheel in the wind. At the gate you join an unmade road between walls. The track reaches the head of a metalled lane beside the old farm of Bull Pot. Here you are on the edge of the Leck Head Site of Special Scientific Interest and beneath your feet are as many as 45 miles of cave passages. Bull Pot of the Witches, just beyond the farm buildings, gives access to this system and there is an information map affixed to the wall of the farm. This is the base for the Red Rose Caving and Potholing Club and for Cave Rescue.

Return to the lane and walk along it. The view extends out to the Forest of Bowland fells. Continue until a footpath goes to the right just before reaching the farm at Gale Garth and swing slowly up in a wide curve, along a wettish path with, in summer, much flowering tormentil and butterwort, around the embayment to come up to the ridge below the top of Brownthwaite. The view astonishes! Of all the many fine views in the North-West this is, undoubtedly, among the best. It extends from Bowland, across Morecambe Bay to Black Combe, and through the central fells of Lakeland with all the nearer hills etched against them.

Drop down the track now and eventually bear left along an old green lane between walls. A long straight brings you down to a lane. Turn right and go steeply down the bank. Round the bends and through a small wood a bridleway crosses. Turn right along Bents Lane and, at the third field to the left, go left through the gate (there is no sign). Cross diagonally right to a stone stile over the wall by a spring and continue on the same line up the brow to a wall and move right along it through two fields to a track. Go left and almost immediately to the right behind the house at Langthwaite. Follow the fence to the track behind Hole House.

Beyond the gate bear up right past a spring and find a gate in the narrow angle of the field. Go left through the gate and cross another field to a wicket gate and go over the beck and through the garden beside the gable end of Fell Garth. Directly across the lane a rather decrepit gate gives access to a path along the right-hand boundary and a wooden gate set a little to the right in the hedge beyond the end of the fence. Go foward for two fields and then veer right to a line of old ashes and oaks to find a stile into the wood behind the house at Whelprigg. Cross to a gate on the far side of the driveway, keep right of the big oak ahead at the top of the rise and bear left on a faint path to the left-hand corner of the field. Walk through the gate and left on a track towards Low Bank.

Use the squeeze stile to the right before the buildings and then go left to the wicket gate in the corner; cross the field to a lane. Cross to a gate and follow the footpath sign for Town End by going diagonally left to a kissing-gate and through by a house garage to a lane. At the road go right into the village past the village hall, the shop, and the Reading Room, dated 1884. Turn right to return to the start.

22 Dent
The Sun Inn

The town of Dent is the centre for the valley of the river Dee, a unique landscape of hedged fields and sweeping fells in the north-west of the Yorkshire Dales National Park. Indeed, this is still, in many ways a part of Yorkshire – even if it is administered as part of South Lakeland District. The narrow and cobbled main street of the town, with its close-packed stone cottages, is a great tourist attraction and the whole is a Conservation Area. As nearly in the middle as you could imagine is the Sun Inn with 'The best ale under the sun' from its own Dent Brewery. Its snugly beamed interior has been serving ale since the 17th century and remains deservedly popular.

Food is available from 12 noon to 2 pm Mondays to Fridays and on Sunday, and from 6.30 pm to 8.30 pm in the summer; on Saturdays service is all day. Winter hours are 7 pm to 8.30 pm in the evening and there is no service on Saturday between 3 pm and 7 pm. Snacks and meals in the bar cover the usual range of fare with the addition of home made pasties. The children's menu unusually offers smaller portions of pasty, Cumberland sausage and steak and kidney pie rather than the ubiquitous burger.

Bar times are 11 am to 2.30 pm and 7 pm to 11 pm Monday to

Thursday, on Fridays evening opening is at 6.15 pm. Saturday is full day opening from 11 am to 11 pm while on Sunday hours are 12 noon to 3 pm and 7 pm to 10.30 pm. Dent bitter, Ramsbottom strong ale, and Awd Tup, their own brews, are joined by Tetley mild. Carlsberg and Castlemaine lagers, Guinness, and Gaymer's Old English cider are also on draught. Children are welcome until about 9 pm. A beer garden is situated behind the pub. Bed and breakfast accommodation is available. Telephone: 01539 625208.

How to get there: The easiest approach is up the valley from Sedbergh. There are also fell roads from the A684 at Garsdale Head, B6255 at Newby Head Moss, A65 at Ingleton and A683 at Barbon.

Parking: There is only a very small car park at the pub. A Yorkshire Dales National Park car park is only a few yards away at the west end of the town and there is informal parking by the river bridge below the church.

Length of the walk: 4½ miles. Map: OS Landranger 98 Wensleydale and Wharfedale (inn GR 700860).

Half of the walk follows the bank of the river Dee, the other half is part way up the southern side of the valley. It is easy going with no steep climbs or, indeed, lengthy rises. The views are delightfully enriched by the hedges (unusual in the Yorkshire Dales) and the variety of trees and shrubs in them. Wildlife is abundant. The village itself is very attractive and has an interesting and historic church. In the past the area was noted for hand-knitting done at home.

The Walk

Start through the alley over the street, just to the left of the pub door, and walk through into the churchyard of St Andrew. Its 900th anniversary was celebrated in 1980 and it still has a blocked doorway and a couple of octagonal pillars from the original building. The box pews and the pulpit are 17th century. A special glory is the chancel floor of polished limestone in which the fossils can be clearly seen. Leave the church and turn to the left; in the churchyard are an old square dovecot, with a pyramidal roof, and the former grammar school, now converted into flats.

Drop down the brow, past old cottages, to Church bridge over the river Dee and take the path to the left on the nearside and follow this downstream. This is part of the long-distance Dales Way footpath. This is very easy and pleasant walking with excellent views up and down the valley and usually a great variety of wildlife to be seen. Hard to the

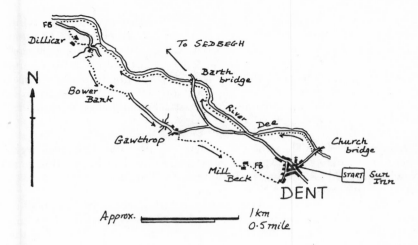

left are the top of Whernside, part of the 'Three Peaks' walk and High Pike, from which paragliders launch themselves into the updraught out of Deepdale. The river is lined with ash, sycamore, thorn, willow, elm and hazel with climbing wild roses and the feathery white blossoms of gean (bird cherry). Pied wagtails, swallows, robins, warblers, tree pipits and dippers will accompany your summer wanderings. The hedges and walls mark out a constant pattern along the valley sides of small fields in the bottom, larger and longer ones running up the slope above them, and large enclosures as you reach the upper slopes and the fell land. By a caravan site join the road from Dent for a few yards and then turn back into the fields after the bend.

At the first bridge, Barth bridge, cross the road on the sign for Ellers and continue downstream. Ahead, and up to the left, lies Combe Scar, an old quarry, and an area of grouse moor. The hedges are still carefully laid here and the banks abound with wild garlic in spring.

Eventually you will reach a lane below the farm of Dillicar where there is both a ford and a footbridge. Turn left and use the up and over stile to the right in a few yards (there is no sign). Bear up and walk over the brow through the buildings of Dillicar and drop to rejoin the lane. Walk right to the barn by the beck and take the path to the right, on the far side of the barn, signed Bower Bank. Follow the track left over a culvert and zigzag on concreted runs up the bank and pass the ruin of Raw Banks just beyond a large horse chestnut tree. Bear half-left to a steel gate and pass through onto a track which passes Bower Bank and a barn conversion. The view up valley to Whernside is especially fine from here. Drop down to the lane and turn right, past Underwood and the fine stone roof at Foulsyke, to the hamlet of Gawthrop.

Cross over the bridge and pass the T-junction to turn right on the signed path up a surfaced track. Go past the old farmhouse on the right, with the pigeon holes over the porch, on the lower track to follow through a series of gates and continue along the top of the first field to a stile. Keep straight ahead and drop down to the buildings of Mill Beck and continue between the barns to an arrowed path to Flinter Beck and cross the footbridge to make your way behind the village, aiming just above the house with a large copper beech and a wellingtonia in its garden. Turn left along the lane and drop down to the Green past the Zion chapel of 1835. Turn to the right and join the cobbled main street. Return left to the pub past a fountain, made from a huge block of pink Shap granite, which is a memorial to the locally born Adam Sedgwick, a pioneer of British geology.

23 Sedbergh
The Dalesman

The Dalesman stands directly on the narrow main street on the corner of Howgill Lane. The mellow sandstone of its walls is set off by hanging baskets of flowers and the bright colours of the sun umbrellas at the few tables which can be squeezed into a corner of the pavement. The building has served many trades in its 350 years – stabling, a saddler's, and a barber's, at least. All is entirely typical of the extreme western corner of what used to be Yorkshire and the whole town is sturdily independent in its outlook on the world.

The day's menu starts here with breakfast (including black pudding, if you want it) for the cooks are also the resident proprietors. The menu for bar and restaurant is an excellent one with a goodly selection of local ingredients and home-made dishes. Particular favourites are duck, the lamb chops, and salmon. The children's menu takes the typically robust and Yorkshire approach of offering some substantial choices in appropriate portions. Vegetarians will find they have a reasonable choice here.

Tetley, Burton, and Theakston bitters as well as Tetley dark mild are served on draught in this freehouse. These are complemented by Carlsberg and Castlemaine lagers, Guinness, and Strongbow cider. There

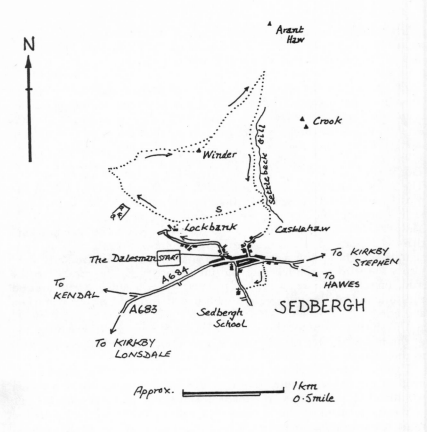

N

is a good range of wines. Monday to Saturday the bar is open between 11 am and 3 pm and from 5.30 pm to 11 pm. On Sunday evening closing is at 10.30 pm. There is an area inside for families but space restrictions make it impractical to allow dogs on the premises. Accommodation is available.

Telephone: 015396 21183.

How to get there: The inn is on the A683 at the western end of town, on the left, just before the one-way system starts. M6 junction 37 is 5 miles west.

Parking: There is very limited parking at the pub. Council car parks are to be found within a short distance in the town centre at Joss Lane and by the Old Library below the church.

Length of the walk: 4½ miles – the shortened route (marked S on the sketch map) is 2½ miles. Map: OS Landranger 97 Kendal and Morecambe and 98 Wensleydale and Wharfedale (inn GR 657921).

The walk combines some of the finest views in the county with a look at the old market town of Sedbergh. The climb up to the summit of Winder is an exhausting one and requires considerable, if steady, effort which will be well rewarded. Alternatively, it is possible to avoid this by contouring along the bottom of the fell.

The Walk

The route commences with a gradual ascent of the lower slopes of the most south-westerly summit of the Howgill fells, Winder. Turn to the right from the pub door, go up Howgill Lane and pass the Victorian Masonic Hall and the sports field and rise to the houses at Havera where there is an old red telephone box. Just beyond, by the 30 mile an hour sign, bear right up the access to Lockbank at the 'Permissive Path' sign. Cross the yard to the fell gate and immediately go left, parallel to the wall, on a green track, which is the permissive path, and rise around the shoulder of the hill over closely grazed turf and beneath bracken and gorse.

The shorter route for those who either lack the time to reach the top of the hill, or prefer to avoid the steep climb, contours above the wall to the right to reach Settlebeck Gill by the waterfall.

There is a steady pull up the brow. At the top turn half-right and then keep to the left-hand route amongst the bracken to go above a mixed woodland on your left. Cross three streams in quick succession.

You now stand at the bottom of a valley which sweeps up to the right towards the summit of Winder. Immediately to the left a wall right-angles downwards and a gate marks where a bridletrack comes up onto the hill. Turn to the right and follow the fainter green track in steep zigzags up onto the left-hand ridge. Once up on the ridge itself the view opens out to the north-west and west. The M6 is just visible snaking towards the gorge of the Lune. Down in the valley the viaduct of the old railway crosses the river and Firbank fell rises beyond it. Here, on 13 June 1652, George Fox preached to over 1,000 people and set the seal on the foundation of the Quaker movement.

As you climb up, the summit of Arant Haw dominates the Crosdale beck to your left. Underfoot is poor bent grass and sedge and the occasional patch of heath, bare soil and rock. Here and there is a block of erratic stone, dropped by the retreating ice, on which sheep rub themselves to leave a greasy polish on the edges. Pipits rise from the grasses and sing high overhead. The final stretch to the summit (1,551 ft) is also on a permissive path. If you prefer, you can keep a little lower and contour round to rejoin the path to Arant Haw beyond the summit. The view is clear from the summit eastwards to Baugh (pronounced 'boar') fell which usually catches the first of the winter snows.

From the summit, descend slightly towards the broad hause to the north-east. Ignore the first path off to your right (which will land you on top of a near cliff and very steep slope which is dangerous when wet) and continue and rise a little off the hause before turning right to drop down into Settlebeck Gill below the twin summits of Crook. Follow the beck downwards to below the nab end of Winder by a waterfall and gate into the fields; at this point you rejoin a public footpath and the short route. Go down to a stile to join a track by an old flag-roofed barn. To the left is Castlehaw, the remains of the motte and bailey castle which defended this valley. Pass the farm and use the track to the right to join to the top of Joss Lane by a house called Moorside. Continue down the lane to the car park and toilets in the centre of the town and turn to the left to the Yorkshire Dales National Park Information Centre; this is well worth a visit, if at all possible.

The stone setts (paving blocks) of Main Street are a great feature of the little town and are, equally, a continual problem when wet or icy. Old stone cottages crowd together along the street. Walk left from the Information Centre to the corner of Back Lane, or short cut through a tiny dog-leg alley, and go a few yards along to the house with two cannons propped up against the wall and now embedded in the pavement; they are a relic of the 1745 rising, when Bonnie Prince Charlie's troops passed this way. Go back to the corner of the playing-field across the road and take the track between it and the houses and pass through the field at the far end to rise slightly to the access road to Winder House, a boarding house for Sedbergh School.

Turn to the right along Winder Drive to emerge onto Loftus Hill opposite the chapel of the school. Sedbergh School was founded in 1525 by Thomas Lupton, who became Provost of Eton College. The very fine library, built in 1716, is on the right as you walk down Loftus Hill to the car park. Beyond the library turn to the right, into the other end of Back Lane and take the first alleyway on your left, called Weavers' Yard. Within the yard is the massive chimney at the back of Webster's chemist shop. Bonnie Prince Charlie is reputed to have hidden inside it. Walk through into Main Street and turn to the left and cross the top of Finkle Street to the parish church of St Andrew. Originally a Norman foundation, it has been altered and added to extensively over the years but still retains a wholeness. On leaving the church go left and take a few further steps to the fine Georgian Evans House, with its superb door surround. The Dalesman lies directly across the street on the diagonally opposite corner.

Patterdale
The White Lion Inn

The White Lion is one of the strangest pub buildings in all the North. From across the river it looks, for all the world, like an oddly shaped ship stranded between river and fell; it is extremely long, tall, and narrow. How old it may be no one seems to know. The story is that it was here that Wordsworth heard of the outcome of the Battle of Trafalgar in 1805 and its stone floors, beamed ceilings and open fireplaces seem to indicate that it was not new then. The more modern climbing boot suspended in the bar is a talking point of equally obscure origins but certainly symbolises the fell walking and climbing heritage which Wordsworth was so instrumental in encouraging by opening people's eyes to the magnificence of the surrounding landscape.

Food is available all day, every day, from 8 am to 9.45 pm; the bar menu is served from 12 noon. The inn's speciality is sirloin steak on a hot sizzling platter and they serve a great variety of pork, beef, chicken and duck as well as fish dishes. Sorbets, liqueur ices, ice cream, and gateaux are always available for sweet. Snacks include jacket potatoes and pizzas.

The bar is also open all day, each day, until 11 pm (10.30 pm on Sundays). Boddingtons and Castle Eden beers are carried as well as

Guinness and Murphy's stouts, and Stella Artois and Heineken lagers; Scrumpy Jack cider is on draught. Children and well-behaved dogs are most welcome. Accommodation is available.
Telephone: 017684 82214.

How to get there: The inn is on the A592 at the southern end of the village.

Parking: A substantial car park is across the road; please ask at the bar before leaving your car. There is also a Council car park a couple of minutes' walk along the road towards Glenridding.

Length of the walk: 4 miles. The route can be shortened by 1 mile by back-tracking a little from behind Silver Crag and using the path marked S on the sketch map. Map: OS Landranger 90 Penrith, Keswick and Ambleside (inn GR 394402).

Ullswater is the third of the large lakes which is at least partly in the south of the county (see also Walks 6 and 11), and is thought, by many, to be the finest in the whole of Lakeland. The steep fells crowd around the shore and its quiet surface reflects the surrounding woods, fields, and peaks. It is particularly attractive in winter and autumn. The walk is a very easy one but does have a steep and stony descent from Silver Crag. This can be avoided by using the shortened route. There is much evidence of past mining and other history to be seen.

The Walk
Turn in the direction of Ambleside from the pub door and walk along to the first lane to the left and go over the bridge across Goldrill beck. Immediately on the far side, a footpath strikes left downstream. Go as far as the first stile and bear to the right around a rocky knoll with trees on its summit, and cross the field. Go over a beck and head for the farm buildings to the left. Your path rises up a ramp to join a track just outside the farm gate. Do not go through this, but turn sharply to the right and contour along below some cottages as far as a gate by a wall beneath the trees in the little hamlet of Rooking, with the view ahead up Deepdale and to Red Screes above Kirkstone. Swing hard to the left and go through the fell gate to cross the beck again on a path signed to Angle Tarn. A mere 20 yards up this, bear to the left along a bridleway which contours across the slope behind the cottages and shortly passes a quarry on the right.
   A fine view across the valley opens up to the left. Grisedale runs south-westwards behind Patterdale village, with the knife-edge ridge of Striding Edge to its right leading up to the summit of Helvellyn. On

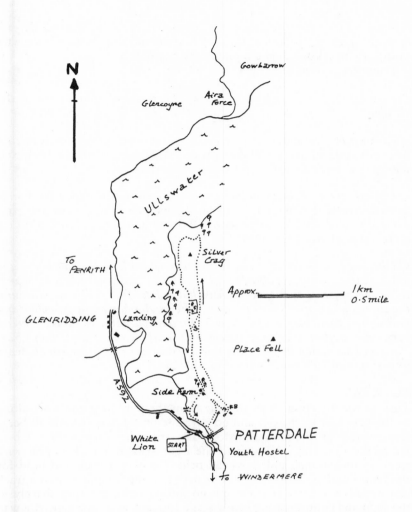

the right, at the mouth of the valley, Patterdale Hall is visible at the border of the woods. This is the early 19th century successor to the hall which was the home of the Mounseys, the 'Kings' of Patterdale. They were so named after leading a successful defence of the valley against a band of marauding Scots in 1648. Between the Hall and the river stands the church of St Patrick, for this is really 'Patrick's dale', the Saint reputedly having baptised folk here on his wanderings through Cumbria after having been shipwrecked on the coast at the mouth of the river Duddon. Continue over, or round, the spoil heap above Side farm and continue gently along the side of Place Fell. Bear up the fell slightly and make your way past a group of conifers below. The shorter route can be chosen here by taking the path which comes up from the left: move on three paragraphs for this route.

By now you will be able to see the landing stages at Glenridding for the steamers which ply the lake in summer. Behind the village is the Greenside valley with the remains of the largest lead mining enterprise in the Lakes. The mines were operational from the 1690s until 1962 and have left much of industrial archaeological interest. Early working must have been of lead-bearing veins exposed by the swift mountain becks but later activity was by tunnelling into the mountain. Lead, of course, was not the only product, for it always had a certain amount of silver with it. In the 150 years before closure some £11 million worth of ore was mined. The whole site is now in the care of the National Park Authority.

Continue on to the low hause between Silver Crag and the face of Place Fell. From this point the view changes yet again as the lake dog-legs to the east below. You are looking across the old county boundary to the Cumberland shore. The boundary ran down the Glencoyne beck to the left and then along the middle of the lake. Glencoyne Park is separated from Gowbarrow Park, at the far right of the view, by the Aira beck which plunges down a well-known and popular waterfall hidden in the far woods; all in National Trust care today. These were former hunting parks and red deer are still to be found on the fells, especially to the south of the lake. At the extreme extent of the view is Lyulph's Tower. This is a hunting lodge, built in 1780, but named by association with a tale of a local chief who possessed these lands in Norman times. The story is woven into Sir Walter Scott's poem 'The Bridal of Triermain'.

Drop steeply down the bank, on a loose and stony path, to meet the bridleway from Howtown and Pooley Bridge at the far end of the lake. Turn to the left and walk round the headland below Silver Crag. There is a better view up the lake from the point on the right. Climb up and over the knoll amongst Scots pine, birch, and larch and cross the beck in the wood.

For a short distance there are walls both sides and at their far end is the junction with the short-route path on your left. Continue past the crow-stepped gables of a barn by the campsite at Blowick House and past some old and large larch and beech. Just beyond a small plantation of larch, reach the yard of Side Farm and turn right between the house and barn to go down the access track to the river bridge. Turn left on the near bank up the river – I was much surprised, one day, at this point to find a canoeist paddling by quietly below me! Rejoin the start of the route at the stile. Reverse the route back to the White Lion.

25 Eamont Bridge
The Beehive Inn

The passing traveller, heading for the Eamont bridge, the road into Cumberland and the town of Penrith, has been served by the Beehive Inn since the 1600s. The verse on its sign is an interesting variant which points to the origins of modern advertising jingles.

In this hive we are all alive,
Good liquor makes us funny.
If you be dry step in and try
The virtue of our HONEY

The building stands sturdily at the crossroads at the southern end of the village and, on occasion, can be seen flying the old Union flag – no, not the American one – the English and Scottish one!

An unexpectedly wide variety of dishes is served at the Beehive, including good menus for vegetarians and the children. Snacks include filled jacket potatoes and pizzas as well as sandwiches. Something of a local speciality, Cumberland sausage, is often sold in a continuous length by weight, not tied off into separate links, and can be eaten as a 'Cumberland Whirl' – and the Beehive is about as near to Cumberland as you can be in a Westmorland pub.

Bar hours are all day from 11 am to 11 pm Monday to Saturday and

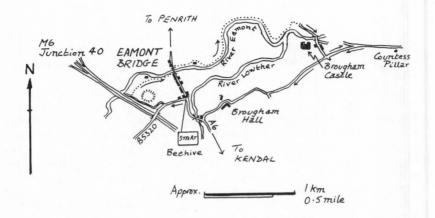

12 noon to 3 pm, and between 7 pm and 10.30 pm on Sundays. Castle Eden ales, Flowers IPA, and Tetley best bitter are joined by a guest beer. Lagers are Labatt's and Heineken, and Guinness and Scrumpy Jack cider are on draught. Wines are available. The small dining-room is made available for families and there is a garden play area beside the beer garden for the children. You are welcome to eat your own food in the garden with a purchase of drinks. Dogs are welcome.
Telephone: 01768 62081.

How to get there: The inn is across the road at the junction of the A6 and B5320 at the southern end of the village.

Parking: There is a large car park adjacent to the pub.

Length of the walk: 3¹/₃ miles. Map: OS Landranger 90 Penrith, Keswick and Ambleside (inn GR 523284).

The walk spans 5,000 years of history. The prehistoric henges are more accessible than others – if without most of their standing stones now. Brougham Castle is well-preserved and Brougham Hall of interest as a craft centre as well as for its past.

The Walk
Cross the road and pass the Crown pub to the far side of the junction of the B5320. A small gate gives access to King Arthur's Round Table.

This is a circular, flat area, 100 yards in diameter, in the field with a surrounding bank about 5 ft high. What, precisely, such places were used for by our ancestors remains uncertain. That they were meeting places of some sort seems a fair guess, but how closely they were related to religion is hard to tell. The English Heritage notice suggests it is up to 4,000 years old but recent work would extend this by 1,000 years. Just beyond is the Little Round Table. The naming is but a fanciful linking with the medieval legends of Arthur.

Return to the road and walk in the direction of Ullswater and cross to the lane signed for Southwaite Green. This dips below the embankment and bends to run parallel to the M6. The verges blossom with white roses in summer and the view to the north includes the southern edge of Penrith town and Beacon Hill, with its plantations, behind. A gate to the right leads into the field in which Mayborough henge stands. This is a massive, circular work of earth and river pebbles, standing about 12 ft high and 160 yards in diameter. From the top of the thyme covered bank you can easily see Blencathra and the Ullswater fells. A single, 9 ft high stone stands in the middle; there were others in the late 1700s and two pairs flanked the entrance gap, to the east. The English Heritage information suggests that this henge is older than King Arthur's Round Table. However that may be, it certainly took considerable labour to build them both.

Return to the lane and go right past the modern houses and right again on the footpath past the gardens to the field on the north side of the henge. Honeysuckle twines in the hedges and goldfinches feed amongst the barley. Now facing east, the peak in the distance is Cross Fell, the highest point of the North Pennines. Pass the black and white buildings at Bleach Green on the left and join the access track to the end of the bridge. This red sandstone structure, of three arches, is 16th century in origin. Look south, down the street of rose-coloured houses built end on end to provide safety for stock and defence against marauders. One cottage carries the inscription 'OMNE SOLUM FORTI PATRIA EST HP 1671'. Turn across the bridge and use the footbridge beside it to enter 'Canny Cummerlan'.

Go downstream by the weedy, smooth, and duck-dabbled waters of the Eamont. Follow the signs around a decorated red sandstone house to an up and over stile and pass a decrepit old suspension bridge. Continue along the river bank with ash, lime, alder, willow, sallows, and oceans of cow parsley, wild geraniums, and dead nettle. To the left is the Georgian frontage of Carleton Hall, now the County Police Headquarters. The sandstone pile of Brougham Castle is soon in view but the river meanders considerably and swings up towards the dual carriageway of the A66. At this point the far bank is known as Westmorland Holme (island) and is a narrow spit between the Eamont and the river Lowther, which joins it just before the castle. Bear up to the left by the abandoned outdoor swimming pool to an iron up and over stile onto an old section of road and bear right in front of the mill and cross the bridge back into Westmorland.

Immediately to your right is the entrance to Brougham Castle. It is quite well preserved and in the care of English Heritage. The keep was built by Robert de Vipont in the early 1200s and it came into the hands of the Cliffords in 1290. Lady Anne, the last of the line, died here in 1676. Both James I and Charles I stayed here. The towers are in particularly good order and from the top of them you can look down on the remains of the adjacent Roman fort of Brocavum. Only the outline of the bank and ditch are obvious in the sheep-grazed field; the site is private. Leave the castle gate and turn right past the farm to the T-junction of lanes. A worthwhile diversion, if you have the time, is to go left and down to the main road and right for a short way to Countess Pillar. Erected in 1656 by Lady Anne, it commemorates her parting from her mother for the last time, 40 years before; the pillar is octagonal, the top a cube, and the roof a pyramid. Return to the T-junction.

Turn right and walk along the B6262 with a rich growth of wild flowers along its banks. At the first junction there is a view of the pele tower at Clifton, across the fields to the south-west. Go right, however, and climb up the bank to Brougham Hall. A large information board tells you, amongst other things, that the gates were originally built in 1480 and that Lord Brougham and Vaux was the man who defended Queen Caroline at her trial in 1820. He rebuilt the mansion but lost it in a wager and it was subsequently largely demolished. It is, today, a craft centre of some note and it is worth visiting the ice-house and the old chapel, which is reached by the bridge across the road. Leave the Hall and go down the road beneath the bridge to the junction with the A6 and turn right across the river Lowther. Over the road is one of the entrances to Lowther Park, the seat of the Earls of Lonsdale, which now includes a caravan park and leisure park, this latter reached from Hackthorpe, several miles down the A6. Continue along the footway to return to the pub.

26 Shap
The Greyhound Hotel

In a county of the outstanding and unusual, Shap is a unique place. For decades it was known best for the notoriously difficult winter crossing of the summit of the A6, just to the south; many a lorry driver has spent an unexpected night here. Since the M6 was opened, in 1971, the village has returned to a quieter life of servicing the local community and the passing trade and has emerged from the dust and grime to display a great deal of unexpected interest for those who care to stop a little to look for it. The Greyhound Hotel carries the dates of 1680 and 1703 on its lengthy frontage and is conveniently situated by the roadside.

Food is served between 12 noon and 1.45 pm daily and in the evenings from 6.30 pm to 8.45 pm Monday to Saturday, and from 7 pm on Sundays. The menu consists of plain and wholesome fare with home-made steak and kidney and mince and onion pies a speciality. A pleasant change are the home roasted ham and beef.

A freehouse, the bar opening times are 11 am to 3 pm daily, from 6 pm to 11 pm Monday to Saturday, and between 7 pm and 11 pm on Sundays. Tetley Traditional and Mild are on draught accompanied by Best Scotch ale. Lagers are Castlemaine and Carlsberg and these are complimented by Guinness stout and Old English cider. Families are

most welcome. Tables beside the parking area at the rear provide an opportunity to enjoy those sunny days. Well-behaved dogs are welcome. There is accommodation available.
Telephone: 01931 716474.

How to get there: The pub is on the A6 at the southern end of the village. M6 junction 39 is 2 miles south.

*Parking:*Park behind the pub, but it is important that you inform the landlord if you wish to leave your car while you walk.

Length of the walk: 4 miles. Map: OS 90 Penrith, Keswick and Ambleside (inn GR 566142).

A walk of no difficulty with only one short rise of significance. A considerable part of the walk is on surfaced footways and lanes and the fields on the local limestone drain quickly after rain. Visits are paid to Shap Abbey and to an exceptional late-medieval chapel.

The Walk
Begin the walk by strolling the length of the village. An interesting, and extremely useful feature, is the variety of services such a small place still continues to offer, even towards the end of a century when so many similar places have lost so much. More or less in the middle, on the left, is the Market Hall. A tiny square building of limestone blocks robbed from Shap Abbey ruins, its archways are filled in and it now serves as the base for the County Library. It is dated 1687 and the tercentenary of the granting of the Market charter was celebrated with gusto. Cottages beside the road, just south of the Bull's Head inn, are dated 1676. Just off to the right of the main road is the Victorian church of St Michael. Almost at the end of the village, and well set back off the road, is The Hermitage, a black and white building of 1691. What was left of the army of Bonnie Prince Charlie after the retreat from Derby straggled past this front door in the winter snow of 1745, harried by the troops of 'Butcher' Cumberland.

At the far end of the village, turn left on the lane signed for Rosgill and Bampton. Just beyond the village sign and the barn a footpath bears right through the gate. Follow the Shap Abbey sign left to a stile in the corner and go down a ploughed field (a crop of beet, when I last walked it). Cross over the lane direct to a stone stile and walk along the next field to join the track down to the Abbey. The view ahead is towards the fells around Haweswater; Naddle Forest on the left, Bampton Common to the right. The path actually goes straight down the field, rather than swinging round with the track past the farm, towards the bungalow at

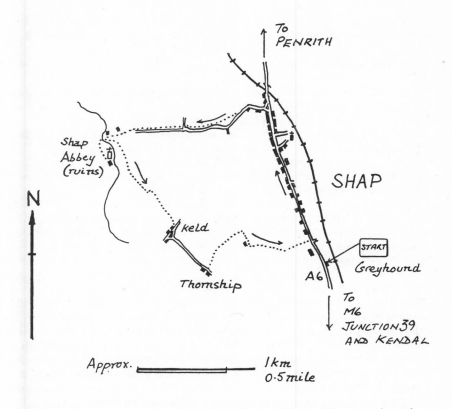

the bottom. Go to the left of this and pass the small car park and go over the bridge across the river Lowther and bear to the left to make a detour to the Abbey ruins. These are in the care of English Heritage; entrance is free.

Only the west tower survives to any great height. This is imposing and was the last part to be built, about 1590. The Abbey of 'Heppe' – referring to the many standing stones and circles in the area – was founded to the glory of St Mary Magdalene in 1201 by Premonstratensian canons, who moved here from Preston Patrick, just to the south-west of Kendal (the next nearest of their foundations are at Cockersand, near Lancaster and at Egglestone, to the east, over Stainmore, by Barnard Castle). These were the 'white monks', so called from their white habits. Every year the prior had to journey to the mother house at Premontré, in the Champagne region of France, to give an account of their doings in this wild and lonely place.

Return across the river and over the access track and bear immediately right to go up the brow and above the wood. Through breaks in the foliage there are magnificent views of the Abbey ruins and the adjacent farm. Over the next stile keep by the left-hand boundary wall, with its crenellated camstones, and look for a set of steps in a rebuilt section which allow you to cross over and then continue on the same line. From the corner of the wall cross to a second right-angled corner and go along the wall line to exit through the garden of a house onto the lane. Turn to the right and stay to look at the little 15th century chapel of Keld – the place of the springs. The key is kept beside the door of the house opposite. Let yourself in and sit in the peace of this place awhile. Down the years it has served as a cottage as well as a place of worship but remains unique in its simplicity. Don't forget to take the key back.

Leave by going back a few paces and taking the fork behind the chapel, signed for Thornship. Along this lane I had the great good fortune to see that rare wanderer a goshawk (or was it an escape – I have no means of telling?). A path turns left into the field opposite the farmyard. Follow the right-hand wall to a short dog-leg with a stile and then the left-hand wall to a stile in the left-hand corner. Continue over the brow to a stile into a green lane. Across Shap village the British Steel quarry and works is visible at Hardendale, half to the right. Further round the Shap granite quarries can just be seen. Their famous stone is pink with the massive crystals of feldspar. Go right along the lane and pass the gable end of a house to an access track. Find the stile to the left at the start of the wall and drop down an old, tumble-down wall to another stile, straight ahead, in the bottom. Rise up the field and bend a little to the left to join the track by the large works shed. Walk up to the A6 and turn right to return to the start.

27 Dufton
The Stag Inn

One of the most attractive villages in the region, Dufton is backed by the great scarp slope of the North Pennines detached from which is its own Dufton Pike. The Stag Inn is one of the many red sandstone cottages and houses around a large green with stately trees and an impressive decorative horse trough with its Latin inscription. The quiet peace of today belies the industrial past of the lead mines which brought prosperity in the 19th century.

The menu provides an interesting choice. Mushrooms cooked in ale as a starter is exceptional and it seems worthwhile considering lamb cutlets in Cumberland sauce as a suitably local follow up. The beef in Guinness is popular as a means of combating the chill of the strong Helm wind which sweeps down from Cross fell in late winter and spring. Both specials and desserts are chalked up daily. A children's menu is available. Meals are served between 12 noon and 2 pm and from 7 pm to 9 pm in the evening.

This is a Whitbread pub and serves Boddingtons, Flowers IPA, Castle Eden and Best Scotch ales. Guinness, Heineken, and Strongbow complete the draught offerings. There is a pleasant beer garden adjacent

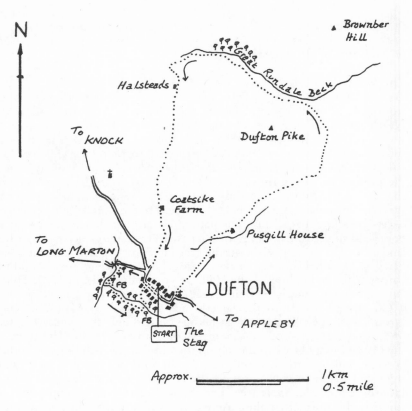

to the green. The Stag has received an award for the welcome it gives to pets. Accommodation is available.
Telephone: 017683 51608.

How to get there: Follow signs from the A66 at Kirkby Thore or the B6542 northern exit of the Appleby by-pass.

Parking: On the green outside the pub or in the council car park at the southern end of the green.

Length of the walk: 4¹/₂ miles. Map: OS Landranger 91 Appleby in Westmorland (inn GR 689251).

Though by no means a difficult walk it is wise to remember, especially in changeable weather, that it can be extremely wet and windy on these fells with little or no notice. The route from the village climbs gradually

*to circuit behind Dufton Pike on good tracks and you are not likely to
find it hard to follow. Views are delightful and the final part of the walk
includes the local nature reserve.*

The Walk

Go out onto the green in front of the Stag and bear to the left. Even
from here it will be immediately apparent why you are within the
North Pennines Area of Outstanding Natural Beauty. However, it
was hardly our modern concept of landscape beauty which attracted
those Anglian settlers, over 1,000 years ago, to found a gaggle of 'tun'
villages hereabouts (this one the 'farm of the doves'); more likely, it was
the patches of rich soil on which arable crops could be grown in the
shadow of the hills. The green is circled by the houses and farms and
they, in turn, have their access 'lonnings' out to the pastures and an
outer encircling 'back lane'. The pattern of farming shared the good and
poor land so that the holdings of the past were scattered across the lower
land as well as the fell. Walk off the green towards Appleby, pass a house
dated 1820 with a statue of Shakespeare (?) in a niche and turn round the
corner with the big house, The Hall, on your left dated EM 1779. To the
left, and facing you, is Lwonin Fyeat (*sic*) of 1648 – the Lane Gate.

Go ahead, now, into the lane, which is part of the Pennine Way.
Drop down slightly along a good surface through the fields; the scar
of Cow Band stands out ahead and slightly to your right. The route of
the Pennine Way bears to the left on the old flagged path but you should
go right and towards Dufton Pike. At the ford of the Eller beck swing
right and begin to climb around the shoulder of the Pike past Pusgill
House. A few crab apple trees line the way. The view behind opens up
towards the northern Lakes. Across the valley purple heather colours
the slope below the intake wall. From the crest of the shoulder there
is a long view up the Eden valley and to Nine Standards Rigg, above
Kirkby Stephen. The track flattens off and the cliffs of Threlkeld Side,
below Rosgill Edge, appear in front. Here are the Dufton Fell mines,
from which much lead was mined in the early part of the 19th century,
though there was, no doubt, earlier working. Ponies and horse-drawn
sleds brought the hard-won ore down the very track up which you
have come.

At the sheep fold, take the gate to the left and along the track which
goes behind Dufton Pike and down Great Rundale. Through the gap is
Knock Pike from which coal has been won in times past. In 300 yards
turn to the right to look up upper Rundale more clearly; the whole seems
a chaos of workings with the remains of an occasional building amongst
them. Down by the stream oaks, alders, rowan and birch struggle for the
sky and the wide grassy slopes seem to hold this valley in a time-warp
of wildness and silence broken only by the infrequent bleat of a sheep

and mew of a buzzard. The slope of the Pike is very steep indeed and is rippled by the terracettes created as the soil creeps downwards under the influence of rain and gravity. The track contours for a while and then begins to drop towards the river and the oak wood on the far bank. Enter fields again at a stone stile and follow a clear path to the junction with Hurning Lane at the ford. Once again you are on the Pennine Way. Turn left and climb up the little brow of Cosca Hill. Back behind you now are the heights of Great Dun Fell, with the radio station on its summit, and the view ahead stretches down the Eden valley to Penrith and beyond.

Soon pass the buildings of Halstead and go ahead along the lane, much overhung by old hedges. Go through the yard of the old farm at Coatsyke and pass a new bungalow. Ignore the path to the right for Knock and the Pennine Way sign to your left and continue through. Across the fields to the right is the isolated church of St Cuthbert. This is another of those spots where it is reputed that the Saint's body rested as his followers fled the Vikings in the late 870s. Records go back to 1292 but it was substantially rebuilt in 1784. In July 1994 they celebrated the fourth centenary of the death of the English martyr St John Boste who was a boy at school here. In the field beside they hold the 'Fellside Royal' on the last Saturday in August, an agricultural show in the old local tradition. Go past fields of barley and down to the lane.

Turn left and right and drop down to Mill Bridge. Just before the bridge take the path on the left into the Woodland Trust reserve. Go down the beck amongst wild raspberries and fireweed and turn left and go over a footbridge to climb the side of a ghyll. Climb the bank a little amongst newly planted trees and take the fork to the left to drop down to a heavily shaded footbridge over the beck below. Climb up steeply, but briefly to the corner of the village green. Go right to the Youth Hostel and then cross over back to the pub.

Brough
The Golden Fleece

The name of this little town refers rather to the Roman fort than to the medieval castle which stands next to it. The township in which the Golden Fleece stands, beside the imposing clock memorial (dated 1911 but perhaps, in part, older), is really Market Brough (as distinct from Church Brough) to which the centre of activity gradually shifted over the years. The width of the street in front harks back to the days when the bar of the Golden Fleece was the spot where many trading deals were struck. The building is probably relatively young as such pubs go, at only 250 years or so, and almost certainly started life as a farm. The inside has a pleasantly modernised decor.

The menu gives the impression that good trenchermen (and women) are expected in Brough. There is a good range of grills and a 'specials' list which has dishes originating from all over the world. A simple egg mayonnaise starter would be well complemented by spicy pork with peppers followed by good English cheese and biscuits. The bar menu carries an excellent range of snacks, salads, and simpler meals. Service is from 12 noon to 2.30 pm Monday to Saturday (2.15 pm on Sunday) and from 6.30 pm to 10 pm (7 pm start on a Sunday). Children's portions are served.

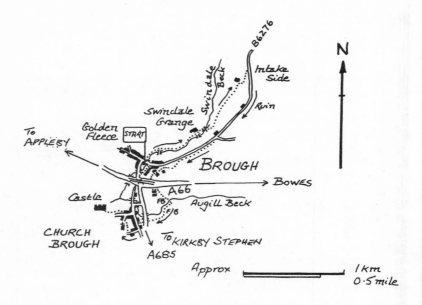

This is a Whitbread house and the bar has Trophy and Boddingtons on draught. The stout is Murphy's and Heineken and Stella Artois lagers and Woodpecker cider are also served. Licensed hours are from 11.30 am to 3 pm and between 6 pm and 11 pm Monday to Saturday and 12 noon to 3 pm and 7 pm to 10.30 pm on Sundays. Families are welcome and there is a small beer garden to the rear. Well-behaved dogs are welcome in the bar but are not permitted in the lounge and dining-room.
Telephone 017683 41314.

How to get there: Turn off the A66 Brough by-pass into the village on the B6276 or approach from the south on the A685 via Kirkby Stephen.

Parking: There is a small amount of parking immediately outside the pub but plenty along the village street.

Length of the walk: 3¹/₃ miles. Map: OS Landranger 91 Appleby in Westmorland (inn GR 795146).

The focus of the majority of the walk is the paired villages of Market Brough and Church Brough. In addition, there is a short walk up the valley of the Swindale beck. This rises sufficiently to give good views over the upper Eden valley.

The Walk

At New Year 1961–62 many were caught by the snowdrifts on Stainmore and Brough was packed with those who did not make it home for Hogmanay. With any luck, you will have chosen better weather and will find no problem in crossing the road in front of the pub door and going right 20 yards to the nearside of the bridge over the Swindale beck. Turn left along the footpath up the nearside of the beck, signed to Mill Bridge. Pass the stone bridge at Sandford House and continue ahead along the track now signed to Middleton Road. This parallels the beck with its series of small, overhanging cliffs and cascades. Go across the yard of Swindale Grange and bear half-right across the small field to a gate onto a stone bridge and go over the beck.

Climb a short bank by a plantation of young conifers and keep along the right-hand boundary, bending left. This is likely to be a ploughed field and so may be muddy underfoot. Keep along the same line by hedge and fence and pass a stone barn, down to the left. Bear to the right through a broken iron gate just short of Intake Side cottage and swing left ten yards, through two wooden gates and round the garden. You may pass the time of day here, as I did, with the shepherd moving the flock with his dogs. Bear right to the top of the slope of the field to a stile onto the B6276 (the Middleton in Teesdale road) in the corner. The view from here is quite magnificent. Far left you can see well up the pass of Stainmore to where Rey Cross marks the present county boundary and the old border of Scotland (the Kingdom of Strathclyde, at least; and where Eric Bloodaxe met his death in 1045). It was to establish the permanence of their power that the Normans built the series of castles to defend the Eden valley against insurgents from the north. Directly across the valley is Nine Standards Rigg, above Kirkby Stephen, and Mallerstang Edge beyond it. The Shap fells close the view to the central Lake District but Blencathra and the northern fells should be visible, and even the hills of Dumfries across the Solway.

Turn down the road and walk past the ruin of a cottage on the right to reach a farm at the T-junction. Go right 10 yards and find a stile, half hidden, in the hedge on the left. Keep to the roadside hedge, gently down the fields towards the edge of Brough. Over the hedge to the right is the folly of Fox Tower, at the far end of the scar behind Helbeck Hall. Down below, the modern by-pass funnels the traffic away from the villages. Pass an electricity sub-station and notice the two millstones used in the farm entrance across the road. At the bottom of the fields a stile, tucked in behind the old stone cottages to the right, leads through a tiny triangle of garden to a lane. Go left and follow this under the by-pass, via a huge concrete tunnel, on a sign to Park House. Immediately go left over two up-and-over stiles behind the farm buildings and bear diagonally right in the field to find the footbridge over the Augill beck. A stream once well-polluted with the spoils of lead mining but now meandering clear through a small valley. Turn right downstream and pick up an old track through a gate and look for the second footbridge just to the left. Cross this and climb the bank and bear right to a stile onto the Kirkby Stephen road.

Cross direct over the road and across the field between the houses to Church Brough. Go left and then right along the bridleway signed to Musgrave and walk down to the gates of Manderley and turn right into the churchyard of St Michael's. The earliest part of the building is 11th century, the tower was added in 1513. A tribute to the commander of the Roman fort is to be found in the south porch, and the cast of a stone remembering a Syrian called Hermes is in the tower. Also in the tower is the epitaph of Isabella Kidd, who died in 1737:

Here rests a pattern of the female life
The Woman, Friend, the Mother and the Wife.
A woman form'd by Nature more than Art
With smiling ease to gain upon the heart.

Leave the church and walk north to the main gate. An old road drops left through a cutting in the red sandstone, but go ahead and to the top left-hand corner of the green and turn left to the entrance path for the castle.

The castle is built in the corner of the Roman fort of Veterae. It famously resisted a siege by the King of Scots, William the Lion, in 1174, and which was recorded in some detail in verses in Norman-French by Jordan de la Fontaine:

He threw at the Scots three sharp javelins;
With each he struck a man dead.

But the defenders were forced, finally to surrender, when the keep was set on fire. This castle, like Brougham (see Walk 25) also came into the hands of the Cliffords and hence, at last, to Lady Anne Clifford whose story of tenacious seeking after her inheritance is too long to be told here. She restored it during the years of the Commonwealth, but her successors transferred their residence to Appleby and it slowly decayed. It is now in the care of English Heritage.

Leave the castle and go down the green to the maypole on the patch of grass at the bottom. The houses and their flower gardens are delightful; Church Brough is, in fact, a small planned settlement which failed to grow as trade by-passed the old road and went down the valley on the far side of the Swindale beck. Turn left and walk through, over the Augill beck again, and rise, past the old boundary marker between the two villages by the wall of a house garden. Reach the by-pass slip road and walk under the bridge. Cross over the road and go up the pathway beside the Swindale beck and turn left, back across the bridge, to the start.

29 Orton
The George Hotel

The George is the only remaining functional inn in the village of Orton. Its three-storey frontage makes it one of the largest buildings and it has the effect of making the surrounding stone cottages appear to shrink in size. Formerly know as the Fleece, and about 200 years old, it was actually renamed after a previous landlord. Internally it has been modernised as the years have gone by and provides a most welcoming atmosphere.

Meals are available from 12 noon to 2 pm (not on weekdays during the winter) and between 7 pm and 9 pm every day. A favourite here is Westmorland pie – turkey and ham cooked in red wine and brandy, which would be well followed by a lemon sorbet. Snacks include sandwiches, pizzas, and filled potatoes and there is a children's menu.

This is a Scottish and Newcastle pub and draught beers include Youngers SB and Theakston XB. The stout is Gillespie's, lagers are McEwan's and Coors and they stock Bulmer's Original cider. Wines are available by the glass. Bar hours are from 12 noon to 2 pm (later in the summer) and from 6.30 pm to 11 pm Monday to Saturday and between 12 noon and 3 pm and 7 pm and 10.30 pm on Sundays. There is a pleasantly shaded beer garden at the side. Overnight accommodation is available. Dogs are welcome.

Telephone: 015396 24229.

How to get there: Leave the M6 or A685 where they meet at junction 38 and take the B6260 from the roundabout; from the north use the B6260 from Appleby.

Parking: There is little at the pub but there is a large car park in the village centre a short distance along the road, or you could park at the quarry part way round the walk on the B6260.

Length of the walk: 3 miles. Map: OS Landranger 91 Appleby in Westmorland (inn GR 622081).

Once a place of some importance, Orton is a quiet village today. The walk circuits through the pastures and up to the limestone plateau above with relatively easy going underfoot.

The Walk
Turn to the right from the front of the pub and go along the footway past the beer garden, then a barn dated WG 1740, and then the fine old farmhouse of Petty Hall, inscribed GB 1604 MB. Just beyond is the tiny building of the former Liberal Club. Cross the road and continue by the iron fence to a footpath to the left before the cottage (there is no sign). Go over two footbridges across a stream and the Chapel beck and turn to the right in front of the houses – former homes of hand-loom weavers and knitters – to a T-junction with the B6261 beside the end of the two-arched stone bridge. Bear left and walk out of the village. The development of Frankland Park, on the right, is in the former stables block of the Georgian Orton Hall, built around a mansion of 1662. In 200 yards, take the squeeze stile into the field on the left.
Aim diagonally left up the field to the gate in the corner and then go ahead to a further stile in a wall. Continue past a converted barn on the same line to join the old Back Lane behind the houses and reach a track between tumbled walls; the scars are now in view up on the skyline ahead. At the ford, go left on the slab footbridge and then go right over a stile in the corner by the gate. Keep to the left-hand boundary to the stream and then go left over a stile onto a green lane which follows up the bank. Willow, ash, thorn and sycamore shade the water and mint, meadowsweet, harebells and knapweed grow on the banks. Go through another gate and pass a large erratic boulder to the left. Cross the stream on a farm bridge by patches of Monkey flower, with red-spotted, bright yellow petals. Continue up the slope and use the right of way through the farmyard at Broadfell. The path goes uphill steadily, passing a wood of pine and sycamore on the left, where buzzards nest. By the gate is a small sign for the Coast to Coast path. Go up to the old limekiln in the quarry; this is now filled with rubbish and is the home of scampering

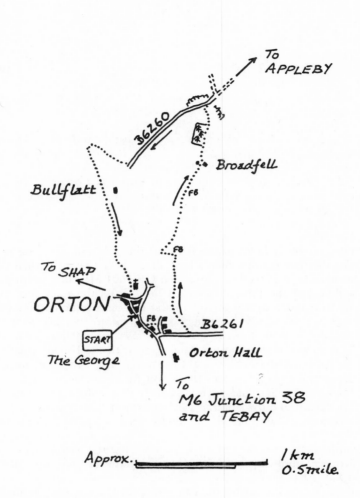

rabbits. Exit through the gate to rise to the B6260 at the cattle grid on the edge of Asby Winderwath Common.

If you have the time, it is worth a short detour over the limestone pavements to the right (the area to the left is fenced off) and to the top for the wide views north over the Eden valley to Cross Fell and to Penrith: return, then, to the cattle grid. There is possible parking in the old quarry here.

Walk down the road in the direction of the village with superb views of the upper Lune valley and its pastures, the Howgill fells, and the Lune gorge, beyond Tebay, where the old road, the railway and M6 make use of the gap. About 100 yards past the steep hill sign, above the bend, go through the gate on the right (there is no sign) beside a small quarry. Rise a little to a view across to the Shap granite quarries and to a gate at the wall. Continue straight ahead as far as the bend in the wall and drop to use the right-hand gap and keep beside the left-hand wall down the hill. There are small erratic boulders in the base of the wall. Pass through a gate, leaving the farm of Bullflatt to the left, and use the stile to the west of the house. After another gate, three more stiles take you across strange, narrow fields and past a round erratic boulder to follow the wall on the left to the corner by a post. Go diagonally left, cross over a farm bridge, and pass a small allotment to find a stile into the churchyard.

All Saints' church is early 13th century with a fortified tower of 1504 and a sandstone font of 1662. It was formerly a chapel of the Priory of Conishead, near Ulverston. For many years the parish followed the unusual practice of electing its own vicar. The gravestone of Dr William Farrar, local surgeon and thief-catcher, who died in 1756, is worth searching out. An earlier, more famous son of Orton, was the Quaker, George Whitehead. His plea to Charles II was instrumental in the release of prisoners which resulted in John Bunyan being brought out of Bedford gaol.

Leave the church by the main gate and walk to the road. On a triangle of grass, to the right, is the re-built village pillory. Behind it the buildings still bear the sign of the Waverley Temperance hotel. Go left and immediately right and along to the square. To the left the old Duke of Cumberland inn has an old Cumberland county boundary sign fixed to the wall. Orton had a market charter as early as the reign of Edward I but this fell into disuse. It was revived in 1863 and a Market Hall was built in 1865 on the corner of the square; it now serves as Parish Hall and a doctor's surgery. The old school dates from 1730 and the Wesleyan chapel from 1833.

An oddity of the village name is that its present spelling and pronunciation, 'ore'tun', is probably nearer to the original 'Orri's tun' than it was in the early years of the century when folk wrote 'Over Town' or 'Sker Overton' or, yet again, 'Overrigg', even if the local speech resulted in it sounding the same. Perhaps the Norse derivation was thought somewhat infra dig? The number of roads which meet here suggests it was a much more important place in the past. Indeed, not only did it have a market, but there were also two annual fairs. No doubt the coming of the road and the railway over Shap fell made a significant difference.

Walk either side of the square and bear right to return to the pub.

Ravenstonedale
The King's Head Hotel

The village of Ravenstonedale is the first across the watershed between the river Lune, which flows to the sea through Lancaster, and the Eden, which flows north to the Solway Firth, and which is fed by the Scandal beck. The King's Head stands at the bottom of the village, next to the beck. Until the 1960s this was a temperance hotel. The pub has been created out of several old cottages which have been almost seamlessly joined together to form an extremely attractive whole, both externally and internally. The reason for its name, coupled with the non-royal coat of arms on the sign, is something of a puzzle.

Food is served daily from 12 noon to 2 pm and from 6.30 pm to 9 pm (7 pm start on Sundays). Local game, such as pheasant, is available in season and the standard menu provides an excellent choice throughout the year. The specials board often carries additional vegetarian dishes. Lighter eaters are catered for with sandwiches and salads.

This freehouse has Youngers Scotch, Boddingtons, Theakston and a guest bitter on draught and these are complemented by Tetley dark mild. Both Guinness and Murphy's stouts are served as well as Castlemaine and McEwan's lagers. Cider is, unusually, Weston's Stowford Press, from Hereford. Bar hours are from 12 noon to 2.30 pm and from 6.30

pm to 11 pm Monday to Saturday (though they may well be open all day in the height of the summer). On Sundays hours are 7 pm to 10.30 pm in the evening. There is an especially delightful beer garden beside the beck and a small garden area for the children. Dogs are welcome. Accommodation is available.
Telephone: 015396 23284.

How to get there: Turn into the village from the A685 Tebay (M6 junction 38) to Brough (A66) road.

Parking: There is parking immediately outside the pub, beside the river.

Length of the walk: 4 miles. Map: OS Landranger 91 Appleby in Westmorland (inn GR 721043).

This relatively isolated place is the site of an unusual monastic foundation and the church is of unconventional interior layout. The walk circuits from the village, down the valley of the Scandale beck – known as Smardale, to a fine nature reserve and the exceptional railway monument of the viaduct across the valley.

The Walk
Walk first to the right of the pub and find the path at the gap between the cottages which leads across a field and into the churchyard of St Oswald's. The church is unusual in its plan being 'collegiate' with the pews facing a central gangway; the whole is best seen from the fine gallery. A three-decker pulpit is placed centrally. Parts of the building are probably 13th century but the tower was rebuilt in 1738, and the remainder in 1744. A pillar beside the south porch may be the base of a Saxon cross so it seems likely that there was some place of worship here before the Norman Conquest. A window commemorates the burning, at Tyburn in London, of Elizabeth Brownber from Newbiggin, for her Anabaptist beliefs, in 1685; the last person to die so in England. Outside, beside the beck, are the remains of a small Gilbertine priory. Founded by St Gilbert of Sempringham, in Lincolnshire (who lived to be over 100 years old), the Gilbertines were the only English monastic order. Only this site, and one in Wiltshire, were far from their eastern English origins. The most recent excavation was in 1988–89, and the parts remaining exposed are but a proportion of the whole; there is an information board on site.

Leave the church by the main gate next to the school, on the side away from the ruins, and turn left across the bridge and then right past the farmhouse to cross the road to a stile beyond the cottage (there is no

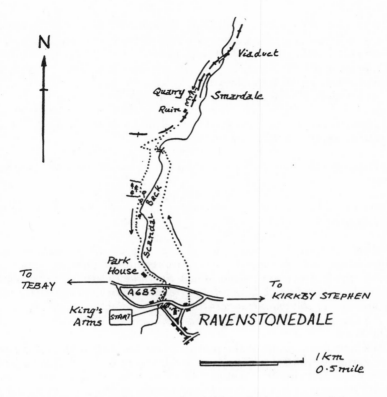

N

To
TEBAY

Park
House

A685

King's
Arms   START

To
KIRKBY STEPHEN

RAVENSTONEDALE

Viaduct

Quarry   Smardale

Ruin

Scandal Beck

1 km
0·5 mile

sign). Cross the beck and go over the field to the by-pass and cross over with care. Go ahead to the gate and the track by the barns. Here you cross the Park Dyke, the boundary of what was, possibly, a late medieval hunting park. Walk ahead to the gate left of the plantation and continue round the shoulder of the base of a low knoll on the right. Ahead is Nettle Hill and behind it, the summit of Ravenstonedale Common at Green Bell; away to the left are the Shap fells.

At the next wall use the stile by the gate and slowly swing round to look down Smardale with the embankment of the old railway on the far side. Drop on the more obvious path to the left-hand wall and follow down to the track by the 15th century Smardale packhorse bridge (this is the route of the Coast to Coast path). Turn over the bridge and follow the sign up the bank by the exposed rock beds of the bridleway. Climb up and swing further round to come to a stile just before the old bridge over the railway, which allows you to drop down onto the railway bed. This is the route of the railway by which coal from the Durham mines was moved to the iron works at Barrow in Furness and Millom;

127

it opened in 1860 and closed in 1962. The whole length, from Newbiggin on Lune through to Smardale Hall, is a nature reserve belonging to the Cumbria Wildlife Trust.

Make your way under the bridge and pass a ruined house on the left and go through the gates over the footbridge. Shortly, on the left, there are two large limekilns with their hearths still intact. Across the valley, the woodland has been almost completely cleared over the years and there are several obvious circular charcoal burners' pitsteads. Pass the quarry face and reach the viaduct; this has twelve arches, is 700 ft long, and stands 130 ft above the beck – the biggest on the old Midland Railway system. If you have the time, extend the walk to go through the wooded section beyond the viaduct and as far as the Hall. This is an unusual Scottish-looking building of the late 16th century with four round corner towers. Otherwise, return on the same route from the viaduct.

The woods have roe deer and red squirrels, as well as the summer visitors of redstart, wood warbler and pied flycatcher. Buzzards, sparrowhawks and treecreepers can be seen throughout the year. Most of the grass is blue moor grass and this provides a sward in which plants like bloody cranesbill, bird's foot sedge, common rockrose and thyme grow. It is one of only two sites in England where the Scotch argus butterfly breeds. Also to be found are common blue, northern brown argus, and dingy skipper.

Return to the bridge and stile where you joined the railway track and climb out over the stile. Turn to the right and keep up the bank. On the right are what the map marks as 'pillow mounds'.These are often thought to have been medieval rabbit warrens but these hills are scattered with many similar features which seem to be much too old to have had such a use. The path drops to the track by a stream. Cross over and go left a little to a stile in the wall on the right. Go above the spring and swing round the shoulder and aim just left of the plantation. On the way you will cross another earth bank which was also, perhaps, part of the park boundary. Continue along the top of the field above the wood to the left to reach the top of a steep bank. Aim slightly left and drop down sharply to a squeeze stile in the wall near the river. Jump over the little stream and join the farm track at the brow ahead. Keep by the left-hand wall and look for a stile right of the farm bridge and go ahead past a small stone shed. Keep straight ahead through the gate below the plantation of spruce and follow through amongst nettles beside the river. Keep down by the river and go under the by-pass bridge beside it. The by-pass uses the old railway track for miles from Newbiggin on Lune, almost to the motorway junction at Tebay. The beds of rock are exposed in the beck and ducks from the farm dabble happily. Go ahead past the houses and the old mill and emerge onto the road across the bridge from the pub.